THE PUFFER COOKBOOK

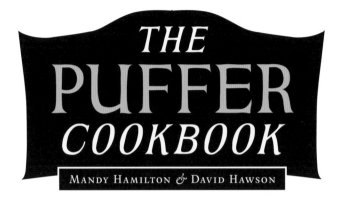

THE PUFFER COOKBOOK

Mandy Hamilton & David Hawson

BIRLINN

First published in 2013 and reprinted in 2014 by Birlinn Ltd
West Newington House, 10 Newington Road, Edinburgh, EH9 1QS

www.birlinn.co.uk

ISBN 978-1-90971-500-4

British Library Cataloguing in Publication Data

A catalogue record for this book is available from the British Library

Set in Adobe Jenson Pro with headings in Boatbuilder at Birlinn

Printed and bound by Livonia Print, Latvia

Contents

Foreword

CLANG!

I have been deputed to strike the ship's bell (once only; multiple strokes are taken as an indication of marine catastrophe), to announce dinner is ready.

I can think of no more horrifying marine catastrophe than dinner somehow *not* being ready. After a day of climbing rocks, tramping through heather, rowing the dinghy or staying on board to knead dough, navigate or fire the boiler, twelve voracious passengers (and four crew) are eager to sit down to the companionable nightly feast.

Mandy Hamilton has shown how to prepare some of the culinary delights that *VIC 32*'s amazing cooks have come up with over the years, and the chosen ingredients are appealingly illustrated by David Hawson (his cross section of a red pepper deserves a place in any still life exhibition). Colour photographs of the much-loved little vessel set the scene for us, so that we can watch the sun setting over the islands, smell the smoke from the chimney, hear the soft beat of the compound engine, taste a malt whisky and look forward to a delicious venison casserole.

Bon voyage, et bon appétit.

Timothy West

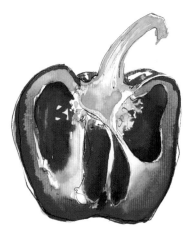

Opposite: Steaming out of Tarbert.

Vic 32 waiting at Rothesay, Isle of Bute.

Introduction

Rachel and I found the Puffer in 1975, lying forlorn and derelict, in Whitby Harbour. After many trials and tribulations and a lot of fun we arrived in Crinan on the West Coast of Scotland and were greeted by the locals as if we were long lost friends. The popularity of the Puffers in this part of the world is renowned and we and the seven thousand passengers we have taken on holiday, over the years, have basked in the comfort of this enthusiasm.

Rachel cooked for our myriad volunteers when we were converting the hold, from cargo space to accommodation for twelve people. These unpaid volunteers stayed on, some for many years, and continued to work apace on board, mainly due to the good food that Rachel produced. Nothing has changed to this day, except we now have many cooks whose recipes you will now meet in this book.

We used to employ girls who worked in ski-chalets and needed a summer job. The poor things were exhausted by the end of the summer and couldn't wait to get off the boat. We gradually learnt our lesson and now only employ cooks for no longer than a week at a time, and as a result the love and energy they put into their work shows, as miraculous and glorious meals come out of the tiny galley on board *VIC 32*.

It's easy (he says!) to cook good food, and the secret is fresh ingredients, love and attention.

The rest will happen naturally.

Rachel and I claim to have introduced the aubergine to Argyll in 1979. We used to have passengers arriving for a six day holiday until one day somebody booked for a fortnight. Up until then we used to know the days of the week by whether we were having lasagne Verdi or pork chops. Rachel had to go into emergency mode and think up a new menu for the second week. One of her choices was a version of Imam Bayildi (the holy man swooned) which, of course, includes aubergine. Baxi, our vegetable supplier in Lochgilphead, had never heard of them. We explained what they looked like and he said he thought he might have seen something like that in the Glasgow market. He duly obtained

some and tried to sell us a whole box as he said no one else would buy them. We bought half the crate and promised that we would buy the other half at the end of the week. However, by then he had sold the lot. Thus we introduced the aubergine to Argyll.

When Rachel was taken away from the boat by a midwife and presented us with a new crew-member in the form of Alice, we had to employ a cook. Thus Rose came and one day asked me if she could cook Arab food. 'No way,' I said, 'you'll upset them terribly.' She informed me she had been round all the passengers and they had all approved the idea. So I made my own survey and the result was a drastic change in the menu from that moment on. Babaganoosh, bread with sun-dried tomatoes kneaded into it, couscous with slow roasted vegetables (thanks Gavin) and mozzarella cheese, tomatoes, basil leaves, garlic and olive oil. These are mostly things which are now part of our daily lives but they have only relatively recently become so. It has been a long, slow haul out of the dark ages.

So, before reading this marvellous book, remove your microwave from the kitchen and take it to the recycling place. Then don't chop your vegetables too finely, as coarse chopping is just as good and the time saved can be spent sitting on a deck-chair in your sunny back garden, or in our case, on the hatch boards, with a cup of tea.

Many thanks to all our cooks who gave their recipes, to Mandy and Colin Hamilton whose idea it was to create such a fine publication and to David and Susie Hawson for their terrific work in illustrating, collating the photographs and providing zest and enthusiasm to the project. The profits from the sale of this book are to be kindly donated to the Puffer Preservation Trust, which is a Scottish charity and has been specifically set up to look after every need of the Skipper's increasing tummy . . . sorry, I mean boat!

Nick Walker (Skipper)

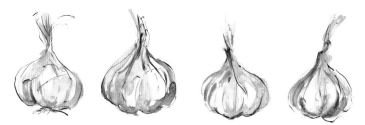

About a Puffer

Puffer is a 66-foot long, 18-foot wide, flat-bottomed, steel ship which used to be a common sight along the West Coast of Scotland. Hundreds of these small cargo vessels were built to fit neatly into the locks of the Forth and Clyde canal. Originating from sailing gabbarts, they traditionally carried coal, building and glassmaking sand, empty and full whisky barrels, topsoil and all items that the islanders along the West coast of Scotland needed. They flitted (moved house) people's possessions from island to mainland and vice-versa and took orders from islanders for small items of shopping obtainable in Glasgow and delivered a month or two later. Carrying up to 80 tons of cargo, they were fitted with compound steam engines and a vertical coal-fired boiler, giving virtually silent propulsion through the water.

The name 'Puffer', however, comes from the fact that the original engines had no condensers and so threw out steam in puffs up the funnel. It was a tradition that villagers came out to help when the local Puffer arrived with, perhaps, an annual supply of coal. If there was no quay from which to load and unload, the skipper would wait until the high tide was just beginning to ebb before driving his vessel up the beach where it would remain until the next high tide. Beaches would have been kept clean and free of any large stones and debris by the locals. The ships were given names such as *Moonlight, Glenlight, Sealight, Kaffir, Pibroch, Hercules* and, of course, if in myth alone, that most famous of all puffers, the *Vital Spark*. It was the Vital Spark skippered by Para Handy, with 'McPhail' his engineer, in the tales by Neil Munro, which so cleverly captured the gentle wit of the West Coast and the charm and cunning of a Puffer skipper who knew the people as well as the coast and islands.

VIC 32 was built in 1943 at Dunston's shipyard on the River Ouse at Thorne, Yorkshire, commissioned by the Admiralty as part of a fleet of over 100 Victualling Inshore Craft (VICs). During the war, she carried cement, ammunition and aviation fuel, delivering these to the fleet as far away as Scapa Flow in Orkney. Unlike so many of her sister ships, she was not scrapped after the war or sold to the far East but was laid up by the Admiralty in Rosyth. She was bought by Nick and Rachel Walker in 1975 in Whitby in poor condition, and underwent extensive renovation before sailing back to her home country. Based at Crinan, she continues to ply the West Coast of Scotland from Glasgow to the inner isles. Nowadays her 'cargo' is the twelve passengers, skipper, engineer, cook and galley slave who she carries down the Clyde, through the Crinan and Caledonian Canals, along the coast and out as far as the Isle of Jura.

Now 70 years old, *VIC 32* needs love and attention to keep her seaworthy. Teams of volunteers spend the winter months, painting, polishing and repairing. A boiler replacement and hull-plating project recently cost £158,000 and a major refurbishment of the stern £80,000. Although much of this was paid for by a lottery grant, further funds are needed to keep this iconic little ship in operation. Unlike most old ships, which are either turned into razor blades, rest on the seabed or, perhaps even worse, become exhibits consigned to the sterile environment of a museum or visitor centre, *VIC 32* is determined to stay afloat and useful. This is the last coal fired Puffer in commercial operation. In the hopes that a plume of black smoke from a little red funnel will continue to be seen against the majesty of the Scottish landscape, all profits from this book go towards the Puffer Preservation Trust.

Morar.

About the Cooks

There's not a great deal in common between cruising with Cunard and a trip aboard the Puffer on the West Coast. For instance, the Puffer has a very jolly skipper, passengers don't have any airs or graces and there's no swimming pool. However, I have it on good authority, from someone, who has been not only round the world on the QEII, but also steamed to Jura on the Puffer, that both have exquisite food. Not posh, mind you. Not on the Puffer. I mean, you don't have to dress for dinner and the conversation at table is rarely about share acquisitions, tends to be on the bawdy side of polite and involves a lot of laughter. The challenge is, however, not only to feed sixteen people with insatiable appetites for breakfast, coffee (homemade biscuits, if you please), lunch, afternoon tea and three-course dinner, but also to rise to the challenge of the 'unforeseen ingredient'; like the mackerel, prawns and squat lobsters, mussels and scallops, the chanterelles, hedgehog fungi and shaggy ink-cap, the artichokes, blaeberries and wild raspberries, all of which can appear, at a moment's notice, after a conversation with a fisherman or a stroll along the banks of the canal. This is the essence of a good meal; things gathered fresh on the West Coast and cooked without pretension.

What makes it all so enjoyable for the cook is being part of a huge family, albeit for a week. These are people who have paid good money for their cruise and yet help with the washing up! There are hardships, I grant you. There's no electricity. So one has to make do without a blender, breadmaker and dishwasher and you have to use what humans have always used to make food . . . your hands. But, in return, there's a constant supply of boiling water as can only occur on a steamship. The fact that you are ingrained with smoke and smuts after a week on board, and need several showers to get rid the smell, is a minor inconvenience compared to the privilege of cooking for such an appreciative audience whilst seeing Scotland from the vantage of the galley porthole, steaming silently along at a gentle 6 knots.

The Galley is the most important part of the boat. Treat your cooks with great deference and always ask them at 6 o'clock what sort of drink they would like.

NICK WALKER

Thanks

A lot of people have helped to bring this book from an idea to reality.

Our thanks to all those Puffer cooks and galley slaves who have contributed recipes: Daphne Murray, Alice Walker, Rob Walker, Rebecca Walker, Mary John, Gavin Turcan, Jock Hamilton, Lyall Simpson (engineer and pastry cook), Celia Goshroy, Susie Hawson and Jenny Scammell.

Our thanks to Alisdair Gurney for providing the wonderful photograph of the Puffer about to cover a pristine Fladda Lighthouse with smuts of soot. Thanks also to John Ironside, who managed to get the iconic photo of the Puffer with the steam train and survived the rather choppy conditions in Loch Eil to do so. Richard Drew gave us useful guidance and Neil MacArthur's business skills were invaluable. Sue Farmer kindly gave us the original idea. Nick and Rachel Walker provided both the encouragement and the vessel on which meals were cooked and eaten whilst steering a course between islands. The seagulls of Millport would like to thank the trawler skipper who so kindly left the large bags of prawns on deck. Unaware of this welcome gift, the cooks had gone to bed and, as dawn broke, every seagull on Cumbrae came for breakfast. It was the only time the Puffer was completely white and one of the few occasions when there was no running water on the quay with which to hose down the boat.

The Trust would like to thank the following people for generously supporting the recipe book: the Murray family, Mary John, Nick and Rachel Walker, Sarah Walker, Simon and Lizzy Judson, Colin and Mandy Hamilton, Alice Walker, Robert and Rebecca Walker, Richard and Margot Walker, Margaret Knight, David Sillar and Janet Foster, David and Susie Hawson, Fru and Peter Goudge, Chris and Jan Todd, IGG Services Ltd, Susie McAlpine, Roy Fenton, Des and Katie Fforde, Jim Forrester, Michael and Greta Wright, the Puffer Preservation Trust and quite a few anonymouses.

Next page: The Puffer passing Fladda Lighthouse (Alisdair Gurney). 15

Imam Bayildi

The Puffer's skipper thinks he was probably the first person to have introduced Argyll to the aubergine. So, appropriately, the first recipe involves the aubergine. Literally translated, 'imam bayildi' means the holy man swooned. Why he fainted is a little unclear, but it's possibly got something to do with the amount of olive oil used. This recipe makes a good starter and can be served chilled or at room temperature.

SERVES 8

3 medium sized aubergines, peeled and
    chopped into ½in/1cm cubes
4 (or more) tbsp olive oil
2 medium onions, chopped finely
4 large tomatoes, skinned and chopped
3 garlic cloves, crushed
handful fresh herbs, dill, basil and parsley,
    finely chopped
4 tbsp water
salt
1 tsp sugar
juice of ½/1 lemon

Place the aubergine cubes in a large colander over a bowl and sprinkle with salt. Stand for 30 minutes. Rinse and dry.

Heat 2 tbsp olive oil in a large frying pan, add the aubergine in batches and cook over a high heat until nice and brown (it will be thoroughly cooked later). Drain on absorbent paper and repeat until all the aubergine has been coloured.

Mix the onion, tomato and garlic together in a bowl and stir in the fresh herbs. Add a little olive oil, salt and the sugar.

Put the aubergines back in the pan and cover with the tomato mixture. Now add the lemon juice and water and a little more olive oil if required. Simmer gently until the aubergine flesh is soft (about 30 minutes).

Leave to cool and serve with pitta bread and a green salad.

Butternut Squash and Carrot Soup

It's the ginger in this that gives it piquancy whilst the butternut squash adds the creaminess. A perfect soup for a choppy day at sea when waves of nausea threaten to overcome all but a hardened sailor. Ginger is a very good anti-emetic ('prevents sickness'), including the early morning sickness of pregnancy.

SERVES 8

1 large butternut squash, peeled, deseeded
    and chopped small
1lb/450g carrots, peeled and chopped
1 onion, peeled and chopped
2 sticks of celery, peeled and chopped
1 small leek, washed, peeled and chopped
olive oil
small piece of fresh ginger, peeled and
    grated
2pt/1.2l vegetable stock
seasoning

Sweat all the vegetables for a few minutes in the olive oil.

Add stock, seasoning and ginger.

Cook slowly for 40 minutes–1 hour.

Blend or sieve.

Serve with croutons and chopped parsley.

Drop a whole chilli into an old olive oil bottle, half filled with sherry, and you have a delicious condiment which gives a kick to any soup.

Wild Mushroom Soup

The flavour of wild mushrooms is enhanced by the finding. If you have the knowledge and the opportunity, gather them. The best book on the subject is by Roger Phillips, but there's no substitute for going out into the field with an expert. So, it's a credit to the skipper's knowledge of fungi that he has taken passengers on walks where they have been able to collect basketfuls of chanterelles, ceps and field mushrooms and survive eating them. All these varieties can be used in both the soup and the marinated mushroom recipe.

SERVES 8

8oz/225g mushrooms
1 onion
2 sticks celery
olive oil
2pt/1.2l vegetable stock
seasoning
croutons
1 French stick bread
4oz/100g hard goat's cheese

Chop the vegetables very small and sweat them in olive oil until golden brown.

Add the stock and cook slowly for 1 hour then blend.

To make the croutons

Thinly slice French stick bread, cover with a slice of goat's cheese and grill.

Serve with croutons and chopped parsley.

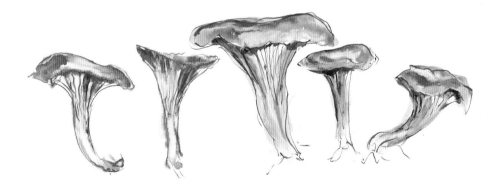

Marinated Mushrooms

1lb/450g mushrooms
5fl oz/150ml olive oil
5fl oz/150ml water
2 tbsp lemon juice
1 tbsp red wine vinegar
1 tsp herbs (oregano, thyme)
salt to taste

Slice the mushrooms into medium-sized pieces and place them in a container with the olive oil, water, lemon juice, vinegar, and herbs. Let them marinate for at least an hour, but preferably overnight.

Place all the ingredients in a saucepan and bring to a simmer. Cook gently for 5 minutes.

Remove mushrooms and allow to cool. Serve with warm crusty bread.

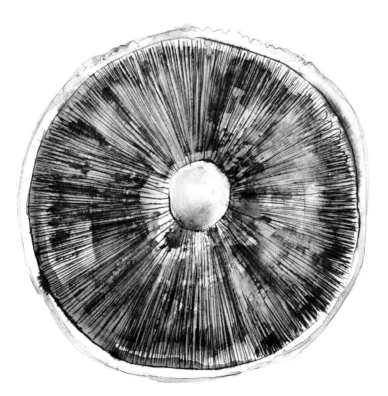

Celeriac and Parsley Soup with Stilton

Celeriac is very ugly, a bit knobbly and rather fiddly to prepare. However, its saving grace is to add a consistency and subtle flavour. This is the kind of soup that people taste, then look up and say: 'Delicious. What is it?'

SERVES 6

1oz/25g butter

1 tbsp olive oil

2 onions, finely chopped

1 carrot, peeled and chopped

1½lb/675g celeriac, peeled and cut into
    small chunks

1½pts/900ml vegetable stock

few sprigs fresh thyme

1 pt/600ml milk

To serve

1 bunch parsley, chopped

6oz/175g Stilton, crumbled

Melt the butter in a pan and pour in the olive oil. Add the onions and carrot and cook gently until they start to soften. Put in the celeriac followed by the stock and thyme. Stir, bring to the boil and simmer for 20 minutes until the vegetables are tender.

Blend everything until the soup is smooth. Return to the pan and stir in the milk. Check the seasoning, reheat and then serve.

Sprinkle each bowl with parsley and Stilton and serve with homemade fresh bread.

In Loch Fyne.

Warm Courgette and Goat's Cheese Mousselines

A dish that's very easy to make which can be prepared beforehand and served at the last minute on a bed of tomato and basil salad. Ideal as a starter, being as light as it is unusual.

SERVES 6

vegetable oil

1 small onion, finely chopped

12 oz/350g small courgettes, finely chopped

1 x 6 oz/175g tub of soft goat's cheese

2 eggs

1½ oz/40g fresh white breadcrumbs

1oz/25g Parmesan, freshly grated

2 tbsp fresh basil, chopped

salt and black pepper

freshly grated nutmeg

tomato and basil salad

12 medium tomatoes, skinned and sliced

2 tbsp fresh basil, chopped

3 tbsp salad dressing

Preheat the oven to gas 4/180c.

Lightly oil 6 medium ramekins and line the bases with non-stick baking parchment.

Heat 2 tbsp of the oil in a pan and sauté the onion for a few minutes. Add the courgettes and quickly stir-fry for a couple of minutes. Allow to cool slightly.

Place the goat's cheese and eggs in the processor and blend together until smooth. Add all the remaining ingredients (including the cooled courgette and onion). Season lightly and blend to a coarse purée.

Spoon the mixture into the six prepared ramekins. Put the ramekins in a small roasting tin, half filled with boiling water, in the oven. Bake for about 20 minutes until set.

Allow to rest for a further 5 minutes. Carefully turn out on to individual plates with the dressed tomato and basil salad then peel off the disc of paper. Serve at once.

How quickly one can change the taste
Of recipes prepared in haste
Like slicing courgettes very thin
And thereby adding bits of skin

Tomato, Apple and Celery Cream Soup

The end result of this recipe is a soup which is much more than the sum of its ingredients. Moreover, sherry is required and should be sampled before adding to the pot. This soup is much enjoyed by cooks.

SERVES 6–8

2oz/50g butter
4oz/100g onion, finely chopped
2fl oz/55ml dry sherry
6oz/175g tomato, quartered
6oz/175g celery, cut into 2in/5cm chunks
4oz/100g apple, peeled, cored and
    chopped
freshly grated nutmeg
small pinch ground ginger
salt and black pepper
1pt/600ml chicken stock
garnish
apple slices
chives, snipped
croutons

Melt the butter in a large, heavy pan, add the onion and cook gently until golden.

Add the sherry, tomato, celery, apple, nutmeg and ginger. Season and cover.

Simmer gently for an hour, stirring occasionally.

Blend, add the stock and mix. If necessary, sieve to remove any bits.

Re-heat and add the garnish once the soup has been served into bowls.

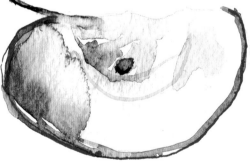

Gardener's Cottage, Jura

*When feeling low it is important to recover a mental
picture from a past, happy experience. If you don't have
one of your own, you can share mine. I was picking
redcurrants in Jura Gardens when a blackbird asked me
if I realised I was taking his crop. After a lot of fuss and
backchat we mutually came to the happy conclusion that
there was enough fruit for both of us.*

NICK WALKER

Jura House Artichokes

As secret as it is beautiful, the garden at Jura House is an oasis of colour on an island of peat and rock. The occasional informal row of vegetables amongst the borders of flowers adds to the sense of surprise. It is here that puffer cooks find their artichokes. Although slightly fiddly to prepare, artichokes make a simply delicious start to a meal.

SERVES 8

8 artichokes
1 tbsp lemon juice

To prepare the artichokes

Snap off the outer layer of green leaves from around the base of the artichoke. Cut each stem so it is level with the bottom of the artichoke. Place the artichokes in a bowl of cold lemon water until ready to cook.

In a saucepan large enough to allow the artichokes to fit snugly in one layer, heat 1in/2cm water with the lemon juice to boiling point. Stand the artichokes stem side down in the boiling water. Reduce heat to low; cover and simmer for about 35 minutes or until a knife inserted in the bottom goes in easily. Drain.

To eat

Pull leaves off and dip into hot lemon butter, vinaigrette or homemade mayonnaise with garlic.

Pull the leaf through your teeth, scraping off the pulp. Discard the fuzzy 'choke', cut the heart into chunks, and enjoy – you've just got to the best part.

Asparagus and Rosemary Parcels

What a delightful change from the usually steamed or boiled asparagus. The flavours complement each other perfectly and the asparagus remains firm.

5 asparagus spears per person, blanched
    for 2 minutes in boiling water
5 parma ham slices
olive oil
5 rosemary sprigs
3–4 cherry tomatoes per person
black pepper

Preheat the oven to gas 6/200c.

Make a bundle of 5 asparagus spears (per person) with a sprig of rosemary in the centre of bundle. Wrap a slice of parma ham around its base.

Place bundles on roasting tin, interspersed with cherry tomatoes. Drizzle everything with olive oil and season with black pepper.

Cook in oven for 10-15 minutes until ham is crisp.

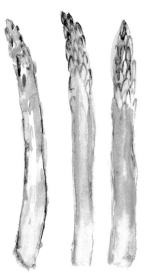
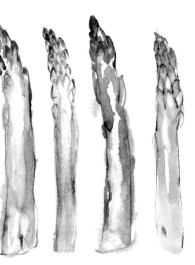

Opposite: Anchored off the McCormaig Isles.

Goat's Cheese and Black Pudding

It might be the fact that goat is mentioned that makes this sound less than attractive; but, as a starter, this is much more clever than either the name or the simplicity suggests. Both Jura and Colonsay are home to wild goats, reputedly descendants of the Spanish ones that swam ashore off a shipwrecked vessel from the Armada. The goat's cheese might just as well come from Greece . . . but for the black pudding – that from Stornoway is by far the best.

SERVES 8

8 slices black pudding
8 slices soft goat's cheese

Preheat the grill on full power until hot.

Peel and put black pudding onto an oven tray and grill on one side until crispy and bubbling.

Turn over and top with the goat's cheese and grill until melted.

Serve with side salad and balsamic dressing.

Opposite: Arisaig Sands.

Puffer Pâté

SERVES 16

8oz/225g chicken livers
8oz/225g butter, softened
1 small onion, finely chopped
12oz/350g mushrooms, sliced
2oz/50g fresh breadcrumbs
Nutmeg, freshly grated
6oz/175g cream cheese
2 tsp lemon juice
1 tbsp (a bit less) soy sauce
1 tbsp parsley, chopped
salt and black pepper

Melt 3oz/75g of the butter in a non stick frying pan and lightly cook the chicken livers. Remove the chicken livers from the pan and set aside. Now add the onion to the same pan and cook gently for about 10 minutes until the onion is beginning to soften. Add the mushrooms and fry a bit more briskly for a few minutes turning all the time. Now add the breadcrumbs, stir and cook for a minute. Remove the pan from the heat and allow to cool.

Purée the mushroom mixture with the chicken livers. Add the remaining 5oz/150g butter, the nutmeg, cheese, lemon juice, soy sauce and parsley and purée again until well mixed. Season.

Put into a serving dish or individual ramekins and chill in the fridge then serve with melba toast.

Opposite: Reflections in the Crinan Basin.

Craighouse Pier Scallops with Garlic and Parsley

If you're lucky enough to be tied alongside a fishing boat on the pier at Jura, and they do just happen to have scallops, take the opportunity to chat to the skipper. For a modest sum, or its equivalent in whisky, it has been known for a bucket of scallops to arrive on deck. Get your galley slave to wash them in cold water and open them by cutting through the hinge muscle and removing the rounded shell, which makes a perfect dish. Throw away the grey, beard-like fringe and ease the muscle and pink 'coral' off with a sharp knife. Never overcook a scallop.

Serves 6

12 fresh scallops, shelled
3 tbsp olive oil
1 garlic clove, crushed
1 tsp finely chopped parsley
black pepper
squeeze of lemon juice

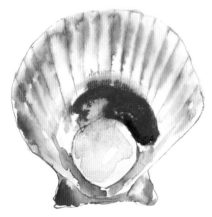

Wash the scallops carefully and pat dry with a kitchen towel.

Place them in a mixing bowl and mix with the olive oil, crushed garlic, chopped fresh parsley and black pepper and then chill them in the fridge for about half an hour.

When ready to cook, heat a large frying pan until it's extremely hot and, just before cooking, lower the heat.

Place the prepared scallops in the hot pan and cook for a minute and a half on each side.

Serve immediately with a squeeze of lemon juice.

Crabcakes

If you've either caught the crab yourself or been given live crab, then the most humane way to kill it is to put it to sleep in the freezer for an hour before boiling it. At the very least, this saves you from having to suffer the 'horror film' scenario of crustaceae, noisily trying to push the lid off the pot. For my money, when it comes to flavour, crab is just as good as lobster; but it has a rich taste which is best appreciated in these crabcakes. Excellent as a starter with a green salad.

SERVES 8

16oz/450g crabmeat
1 tsp mustard powder
2 tsp Worcestershire sauce
1 tbsp mayonnaise
1 tbsp parsley, chopped
1 egg yolk
4 tbsp dry breadcrumbs, plus additional
    breadcrumbs for coating
1oz/25g butter

Mix all the ingredients together in a bowl, except for the coating breadcrumbs and the butter.

Form the mixture into eight individual fishcakes – much easier if your hands are wet.

Tip the additional breadcrumbs onto a plate. Dip each fishcake into the breadcrumbs to coat.

Heat the butter in a frying pan and add the fishcakes to the pan – you may need to cook them in batches. Fry them until they're crisp and golden-brown and serve at once.

West Coast Entertainment

Into one of those orange onion bags, place some scraps of food and a stone, as a weight. Now tie a long piece of string to it and throw it off the pier into the sea so you can still see it on the bottom. Within minutes it will be covered with little green shore crabs. Very carefully, pull it gently out of the water by the string and the crabs will still be clinging on. This will keep your children happily occupied for hours while you watch from the pub.

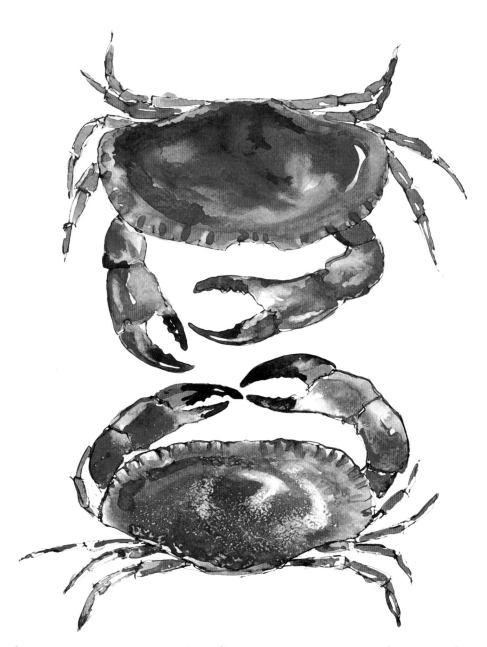

Scuttle, pincer, claw and shell. Nip your bottom. Make you yell.

Harbour at Tarbert.

Mussel Chowder

How refreshing to find a recipe that's not just another variation on the theme of moules marinières. This one is a veritable meal in itself. The word 'chowder' marks this as having come from the States. Despite that, it's good, filling and really original.

Serves 4

splash of vegetable oil
3oz/75g diced pancetta or smoked bacon
    lardons
1 large onion
2 sticks celery
4 potatoes (approx 11oz/300g)
4 large plum tomatoes
1 sprig thyme
1 bay leaf
25fl oz/750ml fish or light chicken stock
1lb/450g shelled mussels
4 tbsp finely chopped parsley

Heat the oil in a spacious, heavy-bottomed pan and gently sauté the pancetta, increasing the heat as the fat melts, cooking to a crisp.

Meanwhile, peel, halve and finely chop the onion. Peel and finely slice the celery in half moons. Scrape and chunk the potatoes; rinse and shake dry. Chop the tomatoes.

Stir the onion into the bacon and cook, stirring often for 5 minutes. Stir in the celery and potato, thyme and bay leaf and add the stock. Bring to the boil and boil for about 10 minutes until the potatoes are tender. Add the frozen mussels, return to boil, reduce the heat, stir in the tomatoes and parsley, taste and adjust the seasoning.

Serve with garlic bread or bruschetta.

Mussels with Ginger and Turmeric

The combination of local West Coast mussels and Indian spices produces an exceptionally good fusion of tastes. Avoid proximity to sand when gathering mussels or you'll get a mouthful of small pearls. Crusty bread makes wonderful vehicle for mopping up the soup at the end.

SERVES 6–8

2lb/900g fresh mussels
2oz/50g butter
1lb/450g onions, chopped
2 large leeks, chopped
2 garlic cloves – chopped
½in/1cm cube fresh root ginger, peeled
    and chopped
4fl oz/125ml water
1 tsp ground turmeric
pinch cayenne pepper
salt and black pepper
½pt/300ml dry white wine
7fl oz/200ml cream (optional)
small bunch parsley, chopped

Clean the mussels under a running tap. Discard any which feel heavier than the others or those that don't close.

Melt the butter in a large saucepan. Soften the onions and leeks. Add the garlic and ginger and cook gently without browning.

Put the mussels into another pan with the water. Cook over a high heat, shaking and turning with a wooden spoon for a couple of minutes until they are all open. Using a slotted spoon, remove the mussels from the pan, discarding any which have not opened. Put them onto a serving dish and allow to cool slightly.

Strain the mussel pan liquid through a fine sieve directly into the pan with the vegetables. Add the turmeric, cayenne, salt and black pepper. Cover and simmer gently. Now put the mussels back add the wine and continue to simmer for 5 minutes.

Stir in the cream (if using) and the parsley before pouring into soup bowls. Serve with plenty of hot bread.

Prawn Cocktail with Malt Whisky

The West Coast has a plentiful supply of these two basic ingredients and the Puffer cook is always prepared to barter one for the other when meeting a local fisherman. The addition of a small amount of whisky does not overpower other flavours.

SERVES 4

Depending on their size, a handful of
    prawns per person
for the sauce
2 egg yolks
2 tsp white wine vinegar
a pinch of ground white pepper
¼ tsp salt
8fl oz/250ml vegetable oil
5 tbsp tomato ketchup
2 tbsp malt whisky
4 tbsp natural, unsweetened yoghurt
for the salad
3½ oz/90g mixed salad leaves
4 basil leaves, thinly sliced

Prepare the prawns by twisting the heads off.

Cook the prawn tails by dropping them into a pan of boiling water for a minute or two until they float to the surface. Do not overcook them.

Allow to cool. When cold, peel the shells off the flesh.

Take a small bowl and whisk together the egg yolks, vinegar, pepper and salt. Continue to whisk, gradually drizzling in the oil to make a mayonnaise. Add the tomato ketchup, malt whisky and yoghurt.

Tear the salad leaves into pieces and divide them between some glasses or ramekins, placing the prawns gently on top.

Pour over the sauce, leaving bits of prawn to show through.

This recipe, when scantily dressed, is known as porn cocktail.

Smoked Mackerel Pâté

What a loss it would be if mackerel were to go the same way as the herring. Being rich in Omega 3 oil does not bode well for their future. This essential fatty acid has been shown to reduce the risk of heart attacks in humans, so making this fish very popular with men of a certain age. By substituting cream for the crème fraîche you can negate most of the health giving properties.

SERVES 6–8

4 smoked mackerel fillets
3 tbsp creamed horseradish sauce
4oz/100g cream cheese
4oz/100g crème fraîche
4 tbsp lemon juice
black pepper
half a garlic clove, finely chopped
1 tbsp parsley, finely chopped
lemon wedges to serve

Remove the skin from the mackerel fillets.

Put the fish into a food processor along with all the other ingredients and blend until smooth. If you don't have a food processor, use a pestle and mortar.

Keep covered in the fridge until ready to serve.

Put into individual ramekins or serve a spoonful on a plate with the lemon and a little salad to garnish.

Serve with oatcakes or melba toast.

Thyme-scented Oatcakes

MAKES ABOUT 20

8oz/225g fine oatmeal (such as pinhead)
2 tbsp olive oil
½ tsp sea salt
3 tbsp fresh thyme leaves or 2 tsp dried
8 tbsp (about) boiling water

Preheat the oven to gas 4/180c.

Tip the oatmeal, oil, salt and 2 tbsp of the thyme into a food processor. Whizz to chop and mix.

With the motor running, pour in the boiling water. Blend for 30 to 45 seconds. The mixture will start to look sticky and thick. Tip in the remaining thyme and pulse to chop roughly.

Gather the dough into a ball. While it's still warm, roll it out on a floured surface to a thickness of a pound coin. Cut into rounds of whatever size you wish. Place on two greased baking sheets.

Bake for 15 minutes or until lightly coloured. Transfer to a wire rack to cool and crisp. They will keep in an airtight tin for two to three weeks.

Three Bean Salad

This combination of dried and fresh beans makes a simple starter and tastes good.

SERVES 8

1 x 14oz/400g tin cooked Borlotti beans
**9oz/250g fresh or frozen baby broad
beans**
9oz/250g French beans
3 – 4 spring onions, chopped
1 tbsp parsley, chopped
salt and black pepper
vinaigrette dressing made with 1-2 tbsp
grainy mustard

Top and tail the French beans and put into boiling water.

Cook until just tender and drain.

Blanch the broad beans and drain.

Drain the tinned beans.

Now mix all 3 beans together.

Add the spring onion, parsley and dressing.

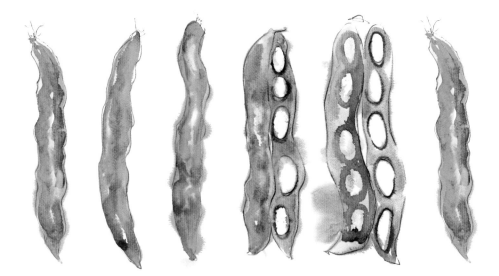

Sunshine and showers in the Sound of Mull

Spanish Potato Tortilla

The most important thing for a successful tortilla is a really good non-stick frying pan. When cold and cut into slices, it is perfect for picnics.

SERVES 6–8

1lb 8oz/675g waxy potatoes, peeled and
    cut into ½in/1cm cubes
½ tsp salt
2 large onions, peeled and thinly sliced
10 tbsp olive oil
pinch of salt
1¼pt/750ml sunflower oil
6 best quality eggs
a little black pepper

Put the potatoes in a colander and toss with ½ tsp salt and leave to stand.

Heat the olive oil in a frying pan. Add the onions with a pinch of salt. Cook them slowly for 30 minutes. By this time, they should be golden brown. Remove from the heat, drain and reserve the oil.

To cook the potatoes, half fill a saucepan with sunflower oil and place on a medium heat. The goal is to cook the potatoes without colouring them. Once they are cooked, drain and keep the sunflower oil for another time.

Break the eggs into a large mixing bowl and mix thoroughly. Add the onions and the potatoes. Season with pepper.

Pour the reserved onion oil into a clean, non stick frying pan (about 8in/20cm across) and turn the heat up. When the oil is hot pour the mixture in with one hand whilst moving the pan from side to side with the other. Continue to move the pan throughout the cooking process. Reduce the heat and cook for 10 minutes. Now take a dinner plate and put it on top of the frying pan ready to turn the tortilla out onto it. When you have the tortilla on the plate, add a little more oil to the pan, turn the heat up and slide the tortilla back into the pan to cook the other side. Cook for 10 minutes. Check it is done by gently pressing in the middle – it should feel firm.

Turn out onto a clean plate and cut into wedges when cool.

Opposite: Puffer among the trees on the Crinan Canal.

Rainbow in Loch Eil.

Chanterelle and Wild Mushroom Risotto

This can be served as a first course when a small amount of risotto is a good way of bringing out the full flavour of wild mushrooms like ceps. Small, young, fresh chanterelles, with a slight whiff of apricots, add a firmness of flesh that other mushrooms may lose in the cooking. The chanterelle season is late summer with a first crop often coming in July when rain follows a spell of hot weather. Rain is not uncommon on the West Coast.

Serves 4

1 tbsp olive oil

1 medium onion, finely chopped

5½oz/150g wild mushrooms, roughly chopped

2 cloves garlic, finely chopped

1 glass white wine

7oz/200g risotto rice per person

2pt/1.2l vegetable stock

1 tbsp mascarpone cheese

2oz/50g grated parmesan, plus extra shavings to serve

Heat the olive oil in a deep frying pan and sauté the onion and mushrooms until golden. Add the garlic and sauté for 30 seconds. Add the white wine and rice and stir well.

Add the stock, ladle by ladle, waiting for each addition to be absorbed by the rice before adding any more.

Stir constantly.

As the rice cooks the risotto will start to thicken. After about 20-30 minutes the rice should no longer be crunchy and the risotto will be creamy. Continue adding more stock in this way until you are happy with the consistency (you may not need all the stock).

Add the mascarpone cheese and parmesan and serve in bowls with extra shavings of parmesan.

Pasta with Prawns, Tomato and Chilli

If you help with opening and shutting the 15 lock gates on the Crinan Canal, you'll probably feel quite warm. If not, try this for lunch. It is delicious accompanied by olive bread.

SERVES 4

2 onions, chopped
1 leek, chopped
4 sticks celery, sliced
2 red peppers, chopped
1 fresh red chilli, finely chopped
3 cloves garlic, finely chopped
olive oil
2 tins tomatoes
juice of 1 lemon
salt and pepper
3 tsp vegetable stock powder
8oz/225g penne pasta
8oz/225g cooked prawns
bunch of mixed fresh herbs (e.g. parsley
    and thyme)

Chop the vegetables, chilli and garlic and cook in olive oil until soft. Add the tomatoes, lemon juice, salt and pepper and stock powder. Simmer gently for 30 minutes.

Meanwhile boil the pasta until it is just cooked. Add the prawns to the sauce before mixing with the hot pasta.

Serve sprinkled with chopped mixed herbs.

Drop anchor in a secluded bay, on a quiet evening after a hard day's boating; standing on the fore deck, listening to the scream of an oystercatcher or glimpsing an otter making his way across the water, is to be nearer heaven on earth.

NICK WALKER

Opposite: Locking up towards Cairnbaan.

Lasagne

A book of recipes cooked on board the Puffer would not be complete without a couple of classic Italian dishes. Most of the Puffers and many Scots-Italians shared Glasgow and the Clyde as their home. In the 1890s, thousands of families from central Italy, fleeing poverty, arrived in Scotland. Today there are 30,000 Scots-Italians. From ice cream to the arts they've enriched the culture enormously.

SERVES 6

Meat sauce
3 tbsp olive oil
2 onions, finely chopped
2 carrots, finely chopped
4 rashers streaky bacon, finely chopped
2 cloves garlic, crushed
5oz/130g chicken livers, finely chopped
9oz/250g lean beef, minced
1 x 14oz/400g tin good quality plum
  tomatoes
1 glass red wine
3 tbsp tomato purée
salt and black pepper
1 tbsp basil, finely chopped

White sauce
4½oz/125g butter
3oz/75g plain flour
2¼ pt/1.35l milk
8fl oz/300ml cream
salt and black pepper
1 tsp fresh nutmeg, grated

To finish
12oz/350g lasagne
freshly grated parmesan

Preheat the oven to gas 4/180c.

Heat the oil in a pan. Add onion, carrot, bacon and garlic. Soften for 5 minutes. Put in chicken livers and beef mince and brown all over. Stir in tomatoes, wine, tomato purée and seasoning.

Cover and simmer for about 45 minutes, adding the basil 5 minutes before the end of the cooking time.

Meanwhile, make the white sauce. Melt the butter, add flour and then pour in the milk slowly, particularly at the beginning. Stir all the time to avoid lumps forming until all the milk has been added. When smooth add the cream and nutmeg. Season with salt and pepper.

In a rectangular, shallow dish (or roasting tin) arrange a layer of pasta sheets at the bottom. Spread this with a layer of meat sauce and some white sauce. Repeat the layering process until all the ingredients are used up, with a final layer of the white sauce. Sprinkle with parmesan.

Bake in the oven for about half an hour or until the top is golden brown and everything is bubbling.

Tomato, Basil and Parmesan Pizza

This can easily be cooked in any small oven by using the right sized rectangular baking tin.

62

MAKES 1 LARGE PIZZA OR 6 SMALLER ONES

Dough
2lbs 3oz/1k strong white flour
1 level tsp salt
2 sachets dried yeast
1 tbsp caster sugar
4 tbsp olive oil
22fl oz/650ml lukewarm water

Tomato sauce
4 tbsp olive oil
3 cloves garlic, peeled and finely
 chopped
1 bunch fresh basil, leaves torn
2 x 14oz/400g plum tomatoes
salt and pepper

To finish
1lb 2oz/500g sliced mozzarella balls
1 bunch fresh basil
salt and pepper
olive oil
3oz/75g rocket
1 lemon
3oz/75g parmesan

Preheat the oven to gas 9/240c.

To make the dough: Stir the flour, salt and dried yeast together in a large bowl. Add the olive oil and warm water and stir with a palette knife until the mixture begins to come together into a soft dough. Gather the dough together and knead on a clean surface for 10 minutes until smooth and elastic. Only dust the surface with flour if the dough is too sticky to handle. Roll out and place on a lightly greased baking tray. Cover with clingfilm and stand in a warm place to rise while you make the tomato sauce.

Pour the olive oil into a non stick frying pan. Add the garlic. When golden add the basil and tomatoes. Season and bring to simmering point. Take off the heat and sieve. Return the sauce to the pan and simmer for 5 minutes to concentrate the flavours and thicken so that it is perfect for spreading on the pizza.

Slide a second baking tray into the oven to heat up.

Take the dough and roll to a thickness of ¼in/½ cm. Place the pizza base on the hot

baking tray. Add 3–4 spoons of tomato sauce to the dough and spread. Dot with mozzarella and basil. Season and sprinkle on some olive oil. Put into the hot oven and cook for 8 – 10 minutes.

Dress the rocket with a squeeze of lemon juice and some salt and pepper and scatter over the pizza. Finally, grate the parmesan over the top.

Puffer Picnic Pie

An impressive centrepiece for the table for a serve-yourself lunch, which is best made the day before. The left-over pastry can be shaped into decorations – fish, shells, seagulls and even the Puffer itself.

Pastry

3oz/75g lard, at room temperature

3oz/75g butter, at room temperature

12oz plain flour/350g plain flour

cold water

beaten egg, to glaze

Filling

1 x 4½ lb/2k chicken – ask the butcher to remove all bones

1lb/450g sausage meat

1 tsp mace

10 spring onions, finely chopped

grated rind and juice of ½ a lemon

2tsp fresh thyme

1tsp fresh sage, chopped

2 tbsp double cream

salt and black pepper

Preheat the oven to gas 6/200c.

You will need a shallow (2in/5cm deep) pie tin with sloping sides – about 8in/20cm across. Metal works best.

First make the pastry. Rub the fats into the flour until the mixture looks like fine breadcrumbs. Add enough water to bring the mixture together to make a dough (not as much as you think). Place the dough in a plastic bag in the fridge.

For the filling: In a bowl, cut the chicken into ½in/1cm pieces and mix in the mace, salt and pepper. Set aside.

In a separate bowl, mix the sausage meat, spring onions, thyme, sage, lemon rind, juice and cream until it is a soft dropping consistency – adding more cream if necessary.

Line the pie tin with half the pastry. Put one third of the sausage meat mixture into the bottom and spread it flat.

Lay half the chicken pieces on top, then add another one third of sausage meat, the rest of the chicken and finally the last one third of the sausage meat. It should now look smooth and rise to a dome in the centre.

To avoid midges, have your picnic in a gale and heavy rain.

Roll out the rest of the pastry and cover the pie. Seal the edges.

Now is the time to get creative using the extra bits of pastry. Finally, glaze the whole thing with beaten egg and cook on a baking sheet in the oven for 30 minutes. Then turn the oven down to gas 4/180c and cook for a further 1¼ hours.

Smoked Haddock and Fennel Tart

An excellent starter or as part of a classic galley lunch. The aniseed-rich fennel beautifully complements the smokiness of the haddock to produce the perfect filling for any tart.

SERVES 8

8oz/225g shortcrust pastry – enough to line 2 x 8"/20cm tart tins

Filling
1 small onion, finely chopped
1 fennel bulb, finely chopped
olive oil
6oz/150g smoked haddock
2 eggs
½pt/250ml double cream
2oz/50g grated cheese
2 tbsp fresh mixed herbs, chopped
Parsley, chopped
salt and black pepper

Preheat the oven to gas 4/180c.

Divide the shortcrust pastry in two and use it to line the two tins. Bake blind.

Sweat the onion and fennel in olive oil without letting them brown.

Place the haddock and enough water to barely cover in a pan and bring to the boil. Simmer for 2 minutes. Take off the heat and set aside.

Beat the eggs and the cream, add the grated cheese, mixed herbs and parsley. Stir the flaked, cooked haddock and vegetables into the egg mixture. Pour into the flan case.

Place in the oven and cook for about 20 minutes until the filling is firm to the touch.

Leave to cool for a few minutes before cutting into slices and serving.

Cheesy Leek Tart

This is even more appetising if you make it into individual tartlets – so much easier to eat from the hand, on deck.

SERVES 6

Pastry
4oz/100g butter
8oz/225g plain flour
a little lemon juice
cold water

Filling
1lb/450g leeks, washed and finely sliced
2oz/50g butter
6oz/150g mature cheddar – 4oz/100g to
    go in the tart and 2oz/50g to go on top
2 eggs
2 egg yolks
5fl oz/150ml cream
5fl oz/150ml milk
salt and pepper

Preheat the oven to gas 3/170c.

First make the pastry. Rub the butter into the flour. Add a squeeze of lemon juice and enough water to bring the dry ingredients together. Roll into a ball. Cover and chill in the fridge.

Melt the butter in a large frying pan. Add the leeks, cover and cook gently until they are soft. Add 4 oz/100g of the cheese and some black pepper. Allow to cool slightly.

In a bowl, mix the eggs, yolks, cream and milk then season with salt and pepper. Mix this with the cheesy leek mixture.

Line a metal 8in–9in/20–22cm tart tin with the chilled pastry. Pour in the filling and sprinkle the extra cheese over the top. Cook for 30–40 minutes until firm in the middle.

You may sing to your heart's content but you may not whistle on a boat. Whistling brings wind and wind brings waves and seamen like me don't like waves!

NICK WALKER

Onion, Bacon and Potato Hotpot

One of the great advantages of a dish like this is that it can be prepared in the calm of harbour then cooked the following day out at sea when everyone needs something hot and sustaining. Variations can be made with smoky bacon or the addition of lots of garlic.

SERVES 4

2oz/50 g butter
2oz/50g plain flour
1pt/600 ml milk
salt and black pepper
fresh nutmeg, grated
4 large onions, thinly sliced
4 large potatoes, peeled and thinly sliced
4–8oz/125–225g bacon, rind off and cut
    into small strips
3oz/75g grated cheese
1oz/25g grated cheese – to sprinkle

Preheat the oven to gas 6/200c.

Melt the butter in a saucepan and stir in the flour. Remove from the heat and gradually add the milk stirring constantly until the sauce is thick and smooth. Add the grated cheese and stir until melted. Bring to simmering point and then reduce the heat, adding the salt, pepper and nutmeg. Set aside.

Grease a casserole and fill with alternate layers of bacon, sliced onions and potato, ending with a layer of potato.

Pour the white sauce over this, give it a good shake to make sure the sauce has gone right through the layers. Cover and bake for 1 hour. Remove the lid and sprinkle over the remaining cheese Now reduce the oven temperature to gas 4/180c and cook for a further 1 hour.

If you have shouted, 'Lunch up', and nobody comes in or you want to sell your house, fry some cardamom seeds gently in oil. They'll soon come running or the house will be sold in next to no time.

Cheese and Rocket Tart with Parmesan Pastry

Perfect for picnics, lunches or as a starter.

Pastry

8oz/225g plain flour

pinch salt

1 tsp English mustard powder

4oz/100g butter, cut into small pieces

3oz/75g parmesan, grated

1 large egg, beaten

Filling

2 tbsp olive oil

2 large onions, finely sliced

2 cloves garlic, crushed

8oz/225g Gruyère cheese, grated

4oz/100g rocket, stalks removed and
    roughly chopped

4 eggs

1pt/600ml single cream

salt and pepper

Preheat the oven to gas 6/200c.

First make the pastry. Put the flour, salt, mustard powder and butter into a bowl and rub in until the mixture looks like fine breadcrumbs. Add the parmesan and beaten egg and mix until the pastry comes together. Wrap in clingfilm and chill for 30 minutes.

Heat the oil in a large frying pan. Cook the onions gently until they start to turn golden and begin to caramelise. Add the garlic for the last few minutes. Cool.

Roll the pastry out thinly and use to line an 11in/28cm deep, loose-bottomed round flat tin. Chill.

Spoon the onion mixture into the bottom of the pastry case, and sprinkle the grated cheese and rocket over the onion mixture.

Beat the eggs in a bowl, add the cream and seasoning. Tip this mixture into the pastry case.

Cook for 20 minutes until the pastry is brown and then lower the temperature to gas 4/180c for a further 20 minutes until the filling is just set and it looks golden brown all over.

The Crinan Canal for me,
I don't like the wild raging sea;
Them big foamin' breakers
Wad gie ye the shakers,
The Crinan Canal for me.
FROM THE SONG OF THE PUFFERMEN.

Smoked Haddock Gratin

A simple but classic fish dish. Attractive when served in individual ramekins as a starter but just as delicious as a main course when cooked in one big dish. Smoked haddock is undoubtedly an unsung hero of Scottish cuisine which deserves greater popularity. If you get the chance, try the most delicious of them all: Arbroath smokies and the best by far are made by Iain R. Spink of Arbroath (arbroathsmokies.com). Here, simplicity and taste combine to produce an art-form of flavour by simply hot-smoking fresh haddock in barrels. Even better when they are eaten fresh, hot and in one's hands.

SERVES 6

8oz/225g smoked haddock, bones
   removed
½ pt/300ml hot milk
1oz/25g butter
1oz/25g flour
2oz/50g breadcrumbs
1oz/25g parmesan cheese, grated

Preheat the oven to gas 4/180c.

Poach the fish gently in the milk for 15–20 minutes. Then drain the fish reserving the liquid.

Flake the fish into 6 ramekins.

Melt the butter in a clean pan. Once melted, add the flour and stir for a couple of minutes to cook the flour. Take off the heat and add the hot milk. Now return to the heat, stirring continuously until the sauce thickens.

Pour the sauce over the haddock.

Now mix the breadcrumbs with the parmesan and sprinkle over the top of each dish. Put in the oven for 20 minutes until golden brown and bubbling.

The haddock has upon his face
A visage lacking any grace.
Unlike the shark, a distant kin,
Whose features sport a constant grin.
Such happiness is hard to find
In creatures lacking teeth to grind.

Potato and Seaweed Cakes

Ulva lactuca, *more commonly known as sea lettuce, is a delicate sheet-like seaweed with broad leaves, easily recognisable by its vivid bright green colour.*

Makes 10

1lb/450g potatoes, peeled and quartered
salt and pepper
nutmeg, grated
2 tbsp parsley, chopped
7oz/200g seaweed (*ulva lactuca*), rinsed
    and chopped
2 tbsp flour
3–5 tbsp sunflower oil

Boil the potatoes until just cooked and then carefully mash them with the salt, pepper, nutmeg and chopped parsley.

Mix the sea lettuce into the potato mixture, then shape the mixture into small cakes approximately 3in/7cm in diameter.

Coat these little cakes in flour and shallow fry in the sunflower oil until golden brown.

Any seaweed that is in direct contact with the hot pan will be deliciously crispy.

To avoid seasickness sit under a tree.
Nick Walker

Opposite: Jura from Craighouse.

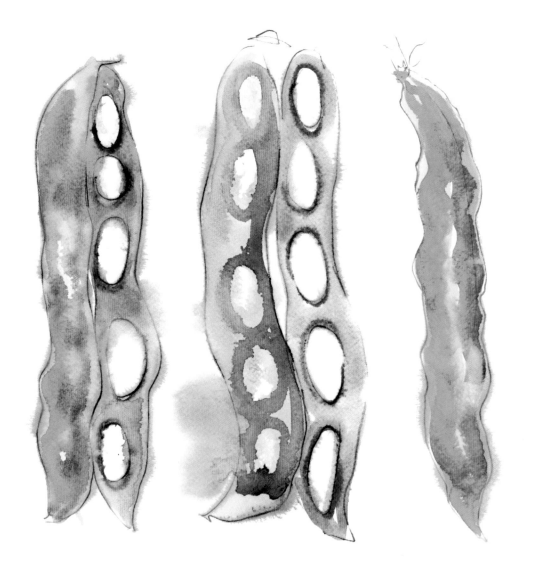

Artichokes and Broad Bean Salad

Think summer, fresh, crisp, sea breeze, azure blue sky, ultramarine sea, no midges and you've got the idea.

SERVES 6

6 artichoke hearts
4oz/100g broad beans
2 tbsp sunflower oil
1 clove garlic, crushed
1 lettuce, cut into strips
4oz/100g fresh button mushrooms, sliced
1 tbsp lemon juice
salt and black pepper

Blanch the artichokes and broad beans in boiling water until just cooked and drain well.

Slice the artichokes and skin the broad beans.

Heat the sunflower oil in a pan and add the sliced artichokes, garlic and half the lettuce leaves. Cook for two minutes, then add the broad beans and remove from heat.

Sprinkle the sliced mushrooms with lemon juice. Mix the mushrooms and the remaining lettuce with the cooked ingredients.

Add more lemon juice, season to taste with salt and black pepper and serve.

When rescued by lifeboat, always remember to say "Thank you".

NICK WALKER

Cauliflower and Roast Pepper Gratin

The cauliflower should remain firm when cooked. Take care not to overcook it. If you have vegetarians on board, this dish can be eaten without the bacon – but frankly, if only for the aroma alone, cook the bacon. Even a vegetarian's appetite is stimulated by the smell of bacon cooking.

SERVES 4

1 pepper – red, yellow or green
olive oil
1 large cauliflower
1 tsp vegetable stock powder
salt and black pepper
4oz/100g cheddar cheese, grated
small pieces grilled crispy bacon to garnish
(bacon not essential even for the most decadent veggie)

Sauce
½pt/300ml whole milk
½ onion, cut in half
1 bay leaf
1oz/25g butter
1oz/25g plain flour
salt and black pepper

Preheat the oven to gas 8/230c.

Start the sauce by putting the milk into a small saucepan with the onion, bay leaf and peppercorns. Bring to simmering point, turn off the heat and leave to infuse for 30 minutes or so.

De-seed the pepper and roughly chop. Sprinkle with olive oil and place in the oven to roast for 20 minutes until it is starting to go brown at the edges.

Boil the cauliflower in lightly salted water for 7–8 minutes until it begins to soften.

To finish the sauce, strain the warm milk into a jug. Melt the butter in a small pan and add the flour. Stir vigorously and cook for a minute or two. Remove from the heat and start to add the milk stirring all the time to make sure no lumps form. Add the rest of the milk, bring to simmering point, add the grated cheese and stock powder and season to taste.

Put the cooked cauliflower into a serving dish. Cover with the cheese sauce and garnish with the roasted pepper. Finally scatter over the crispy bacon, if used.

Opposite: The Skipper with his sun-hat on.

Roasted Vegetables with Couscous Salad

This salad is often served for lunch on the Puffer as part of an array of dishes. It always disappears before anything else.

Serves 8

1 aubergine, cubed
1 courgette, cubed
salt
1 red pepper, seeded and roughly chopped
1 yellow pepper, seeded and roughly chopped
2 onions, chopped into chunks
6 garlic cloves, peeled and left whole
olive oil
black pepper
5oz/130g couscous
2 tbsp olive oil
9fl oz/275ml boiling water
vinaigrette dressing
2 tbsp parsley, chopped
2 tbsp pine nuts, toasted

Preheat the oven to gas 8/230c.

In a large baking tin, roast the aubergine, courgette, onion, peppers and garlic cloves. Put the vegetables in a single layer – if necessary use an extra tin. Sprinkle with olive oil making sure everything is well coated and season with black pepper. Roast in the oven for about 30 minutes or until the vegetables are turning brown at the edges.

Put the couscous into a pan. Add the olive oil and a little salt. Pour the boiling water into the pan and gently stir. Put the pan onto a very low heat for a minute or two. Stir again and then leave, with the lid on, for 15 minutes until the couscous has absorbed all the liquid and is soft.

When everything is cooked, combine the vegetables with the couscous, pour on the dressing, check the seasoning and finally stir in the chopped parsley and toasted pine nuts.

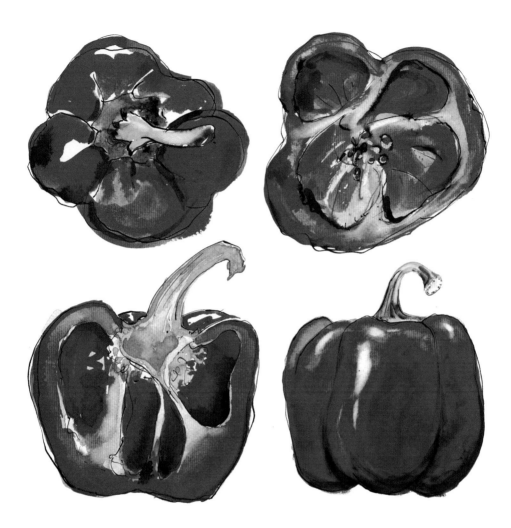

If needing a dish to produce
For a vegan you want to seduce
You can't do much better
Than show her your pepper
Served up on a bed of couscous

Puy Lentil, Spinach and Crispy Bacon Salad

This is the kind of salad that makes the average vegetarian wish they weren't. And if you are . . . you can always substitute feta cheese for the bacon.

SERVES 4

1 onion, finely chopped
1 stick of celery, finely chopped
1 tbsp olive oil
8oz/225g Puy lentils
10fl oz/300ml boiling water
6oz/150g smoked bacon lardons
9oz/250g baby spinach
vinaigrette dressing made with grainy
    mustard

Put the olive oil into a pan, add the onion and celery and cook gently for a few minutes until the vegetables begin to soften. Now stir in the lentils and add the water. Cover the pan and simmer for 25–30 minutes. By this time all the water will have been absorbed and the lentils will be soft but not mushy.

Fry the smoked bacon lardons until crispy.

Take a clean pan and add the spinach and a spoonful of water. Cook for a minute or two until the spinach has wilted. Squeeze all the water out of the spinach, drain and roughly chop.

While the lentils are still warm pour the vinaigrette over them and mix in the spinach.

Sprinkle the lardons over the top and serve.

'Why don't you convert to diesel?' is the most commonly asked question of a coal-fired steam mariner. The answer is 'Because it doesn't stick on the shovel.'

NICK WALKER

Crinan Light.

Tweed Kettle

Salmon, like oysters, were once the food of the poor. Tweed Kettle is an example of a dish for the masses, once prepared in the cook-shops of Edinburgh, where food made in quantity was on offer cheaply to those without the desire or means to prepare it themselves – the forerunners of today's chippies and kebab shops.

Serves 6

2lb/900g fresh salmon – tail is best
¼pt/150ml water
salt and pepper
¼tsp ground mace
¼pt/150ml dry white wine
2 shallots, chopped
4oz/100g mushrooms, chopped
butter
1 tbsp parsley, chopped

Preheat the oven to gas 4/180c.

Put the fish into a fish kettle or pan, barely cover with water, bring to the boil and simmer gently for 5 minutes. Take the fish out of the pan but reserve the liquid. Remove all the skin and bones from the fish and cut the flesh into fairly chunky pieces. Season the salmon with salt, pepper and mace and place in a baking dish together with the water that the fish was simmered in, the wine and the shallots. Cover and poach gently for 20 minutes.

Meanwhile melt the butter in a clean pan and soften the mushrooms without colouring.

At the end of the fish cooking time, add the mushrooms and put back in the oven for 5 minutes.

Sprinkle the parsley over the top and serve.

Always treat customs officers with great respect.
Nick Walker

Opposite: In the Crinan Canal by Bellanoch.

Lamb Tagine

Scottish lamb is particularly good in the late summer. Shoulder is an excellent cut for slower cooking as it becomes increasingly juicy and tender. This has been a staple on the Puffer since the earliest years and there are many different recipes used – everyone has their own combination of spices. Try this one.

SERVES 6–8

3 cloves garlic, crushed

2 tsp ground cumin

1 tsp ground ginger

½ tsp salt

¾ tsp turmeric

¾ tsp paprika

½ tsp cinnamon

black pepper

3 lbs/1.35k lamb shoulder cut into bite-size pieces

4 tbsp olive oil

2 onions, sliced

1 tbsp honey

4oz/100g dried apricots, chopped

2 preserved lemons

25fl oz/750ml vegetable stock

Preheat the oven to gas 4/180c.

Combine the garlic, cumin, ground ginger, salt, turmeric, paprika, cinnamon and black pepper in a small bowl and mix together.

Put the lamb pieces into a bowl and sprinkle on the spice mixture and gently mix. Heat 3 tbsp oil in a heavy pan over a fairly high heat and brown the lamb in batches, removing to a plate when slightly coloured.

Now add the last tbsp of oil and put in the onions cooking gently until they are beginning to turn golden brown.

Put the lamb back into the pan with the onions, honey, apricots and preserved lemons and then add the stock. Stir gently making sure nothing is sticking to the bottom. Bring to simmering point and cook for two hours until the lamb is tender.

Serve with couscous.

Sack anybody who asks you the question, 'Are you sure?'

NICK WALKER

Wednesday Dinner Cumbrae

Courgette & Goat's Cheese Mousseline

Moroccan Lamb

Key Lime Pie

Made with the last tin of condensed milk from the Millport Newsagent

Slow-cooked Lamb Shanks

This cut of lamb is very underrated. West Coast lamb has had to work hard on heather and moorland to acquire flavour. If you're really liberal with the garlic, midges will not come near you – nor will anyone else.

SERVES 8

2 tbsp olive oil
3 onions, sliced
4 cloves garlic
8 lamb shanks
3 tbsp plain flour
5 sprigs fresh rosemary, chopped
3 glasses red wine
1-2 glasses water
seasoning

Preheat the oven to gas 3/170c.

Heat the oil in a heavy frying pan and fry the onions until soft, adding the garlic towards the end of the cooking time. Put the cooked onions and garlic into an oven tray large enough to hold the shanks.

Season the flour, add chopped rosemary and mix it all up. Rub the flour onto the lamb shanks.

Brown the shanks in olive oil in the frying pan. Don't overcrowd the pan; you can do it in batches. When they are crispy and brown add them to the oven tray on top of the onions.

Deglaze the frying pan with 3 glasses of red wine and a glass of water (you can add more water later if necessary). Add this to the shanks making sure to scrape all the little bits from the bottom of the frying pan.

Cover with a double layer of tinfoil and put in the oven.

Cook for 4 hours. Serve with rice or roast potatoes and seasonal vegetables.

Opposite: In the Galley.

Venison Casserole with Bog Myrtle and Prunes

Companions in the wild, it seems only appropriate that venison and bog myrtle end up in the same dish together. Bog myrtle grows in peaty, boggy areas hence its abundance all over the west coast of Scotland. In Britain, until the cultivation of hops in the sixteenth century, bog myrtle was one of the herbs used to flavour beer (heather being another one). Today it is used as a traditional ingredient in Royal wedding bouquets, as a midge repellent (but not necessarily at Royal weddings) and, as in this dish, a perfect accompaniment to venison.

SERVES 6

2lbs/900g venison (haunch or loin) cut
    into cubes
4 tbsp oil
2-3 spring onions, roughly chopped
8oz/225g mushrooms, sliced
2 cloves garlic, peeled and crushed
½ in/1cm root ginger, peeled and grated
1 tbsp redcurrant jelly
8oz/225g prunes
2–3 leaves bog myrtle
1 tbsp cornflour
1 tbsp soy sauce
1 tbsp tomato purée

Stock
1 tbsp demerara sugar
1 pt/600ml chicken stock
splash of wine
I tbsp wine vinegar
few mushroom stalks
pinch of wild thyme

Preheat the oven to gas 3/170c.

First make the stock. Sprinkle the Demerara sugar over the base of a pan and caramelise well. Add chicken stock, wine and wine vinegar. Bring to boil and put in a few mushroom stalks and the thyme. Simmer for 20 minutes until the liquid is reduced to half a pint. Strain into a jug.

Heat 2 tbsp oil in a pan and add half the venison and sauté gently. Remove from the pan and sauté the remaining meat. Return the venison to the pan, with spring onions and mushrooms and sauté for 2–3 minutes. Add garlic, ginger and redcurrant jelly and stir well.

Make a paste from the soy sauce, cornflour and tomato purée. Add this to the venison together with prunes and bog myrtle and pour on the stock mixture. Stir well and bring to simmering point. Cover and cook for 40 minutes either on the hob or in the oven.

Ben Nevis from Corpach.

Highland Venison Pie

The cooks on the Puffer are keen to show off all the best in Scottish ingredients and a cruise would not be complete without venison. Venison is perfect as a filling for pies and this is one of the best pie recipes you will ever taste.

SERVES 6–8

2lb/900g casserole venison – cut into
    1in/2cm pieces

1oz/25g butter

4oz/100g smoked streaky bacon
 snipped into bits

12oz/325g shallots, peeled and left whole

2 or 3 cloves garlic, crushed

2oz/50g plain flour

10fl oz/300ml red wine

15fl oz/450ml chicken stock

1 tbsp tomato purée

1 tbsp runny honey

2 sticks celery, finely chopped

8oz/225g chestnut mushrooms, whole, or,
    if large, halved

salt and pepper

1 x 1lb 2oz/500g pack frozen puff pastry

1 egg, for glazing

Preheat the oven to gas 3/170c.

Melt the butter and brown the venison in batches in a frying pan. Spoon into a large casserole.

Fry the bacon until the fat begins to run. Add the shallots and garlic and fry for a further 5 minutes. Add the flour, stir well and cook for a minute or two. Now pour in the wine and the stock. Add the tomato purée, honey, celery, mushrooms and the seasoning. Bring to boiling point and simmer for 5 minutes.

Pour this sauce over the venison in the casserole. Cover and put into the oven for about 1½ hours until the venison is tender. Remove from the oven and turn the temperature up to gas 7/220c.

Pour the venison mixture into an appropriately sized pie dish. Roll out the pastry to about ¼in/0.5cm thick and cover the pie making sure to seal the edges. Brush on the beaten egg. Now cook for a further 30–40 minutes until golden brown.

Pork Chops with Fennel and Red Onion

. . . or, how to make pork chops interesting.

SERVES 6

olive oil

4 cloves of garlic, peeled and chopped

1 tsp fennel seeds

2 tsp red wine vinegar with a pinch of sugar

½ tsp smoked hot paprika

6 pork loin steaks (not too thick)

3 large red onions, peeled
   and sliced

1 large fennel bulb, trimmed
   and chopped (reserve the fennel top for
      the garnish)

2 bay leaves

1 glass white wine

Garnish
small bunch parsley, chopped
green fennel top, chopped

Crush the garlic and fennel seeds together in a pestle and mortar until fairly smooth. Add a little salt and pepper, the vinegar, paprika and 1 tbsp of olive oil. Rub this mixture into the pork chops, cover and set aside.

Heat some olive oil in a frying pan. Add the onions, fennel, bay leaves and a little salt. Fry gently for 15 minutes or so until the onion is translucent and beginning to caramelise. Remove this mixture from the pan with a slotted spoon leaving the flavoured olive oil behind. Turn up the heat and add the pork chops, frying for a couple of minutes on each side (they will still be pink in the middle). Return the onion mixture to the pan, add the wine and simmer for a few minutes until the chops are cooked through.

Serve the chops on top of the onion and fennel mixture garnished with the chopped parsley and fennel tops.

Mashed potato complements this dish perfectly.

*If I think my crew doubts my interpretation of a
situation, I go below and change my pink trousers to blue
ones. I find this has the desired effect.*

NICK WALKER.

Pork and Blue Cheese Casserole

I used to worry that the addition of cheese, especially blue cheese, was an excuse to hide the flavours of everything else in a recipe. Not so. This works well.

Serves 8

2 onions, chopped
3lbs/1.35k pork shoulder cut into cubes
1 heaped tbsp flour
Olive oil
Rosemary
2 bay leaves
2 tbsp tomato purée
3 cloves garlic, chopped
Salt and black pepper
1pt/600ml vegetable stock
10fl oz/300ml cider or white wine
4 to 6 carrots, chopped
1 or 2 tbsp redcurrant jelly
7oz/200g blue cheese, Stilton or Danish
    Blue

Heat the oil in a heavy casserole dish and then add the onions and cook gently to soften for 5 to 10 minutes. Remove the onions to a plate.

Season the flour with salt and pepper and sprinkle it over the pork.

Add more oil to the casserole dish, turn the heat up and quickly brown the pork cubes. When sealed, add the onions, rosemary, bay leaves, tomato purée, garlic, salt and pepper and cook for 3 minutes. Now pour in the stock and cider or wine.

Give everything a thorough but gentle stir. Simmer for about 40 minutes. Add the carrots, redcurrant jelly and crumble in the cheese. Simmer for a further 20 minutes until everything is hot, the carrots are just cooked and the cheese has melted.

Good served with rice.

The Puffer did once make an effort to be more environmentally friendly. She underwent a trial of burning wood chips. Unfortunately, the calorific value of pulped wood is approximately three-quarters that of coal, which means a lot more shovelling for the same speed. The engineer was not happy.

NICK WALKER

Chicken with Tarragon

The slightly aniseedy flavour of tarragon (dragon's wort) goes well with chicken.

SERVES 4

4 chicken breasts, skin on
1 tbsp runny honey
vegetable oil
salt and black pepper
sauce
3fl oz/75ml medium dry white wine
5fl oz/150ml chicken stock
2 sprigs tarragon
5fl oz/150ml double cream
2 tbsp chopped tarragon

Preheat the oven to gas 6/200c.

In a roasting tin, brown the chicken breasts in a little oil. Season both sides and turn skin side up before pouring over the honey.

Roast until cooked through – about 20 minutes. Remove the chicken from the pan and keep warm while you make the sauce.

Pour off any excess fat, add the wine and bring to the boil, scraping to make sure you include any of the juices from the chicken. Reduce until you're left with a couple of tablespoons of richly flavoured liquid.

Add the stock and the sprigs of tarragon, bring to the boil and reduce by a third. Stir in the cream, simmer and allow to reduce a little before removing the sprigs of tarragon and adding the freshly chopped tarragon leaves. Adjust the seasoning and serve spooned over the chicken.

Never shake hands across water. You must either be on the same boat or together on the shore.

NICK WALKER

Chicken and Leek Pie

Cooks on the Puffer always come armed with a few recipes that are easy enough to prepare for sixteen hungry mouths . . . and taste good. This is one of them.

Serves 6

4 tbsp olive oil

1oz/25g butter

3lb/1.35kg chicken thighs, boned and cut into pieces

3 leeks, washed and sliced into chunks

3 carrots, peeled and roughly chopped

3 sticks of celery, finely sliced

1-2 tbsp fresh thyme

2 tbsp flour

½ pt/300ml milk

1 wineglass white wine

1 wineglass water

salt and black pepper

1lb 2oz/500g pack good quality frozen puff pastry

1 egg for glazing

Preheat the oven to gas 7/220c.

Take a roomy casserole or heavy-based saucepan and put in the olive oil and butter. Set over a medium heat before adding the chicken, leeks, carrots, celery and thyme. Cook gently for 15 minutes and then turn up the heat.

Now add the flour and stir for a minute or two before pouring in the milk, wine and water. Season with salt and pepper and barely simmer on the hob for 30 minutes.

Pile everything into a pie dish ensuring that the mixture almost fills the dish.

Roll out the pastry, brush the rim of the dish with beaten egg and lay the pastry over the top. Trim allowing a generous overlap in case the pastry shrinks in the oven. Now add any decoration you want to using the leftover pieces. Brush the pastry with the beaten egg. Cook for about 30–40 minutes or until golden brown.

Castle Stalker.

Leaking is not to be confused with sinking. The two must not be mixed up. For a start, leaking is manageable, whereas sinking is a term used only in extremis and is usually psychologically upsetting to the mental health of the crew. It has been said that a frightened person with a bucket is worth twenty pumps.

Nick Walker

Chicken Cacciatore

This is a simple combination of flavours that is always appreciated. Cacciatore means 'hunter' in Italian, though hopefully you'll be able to buy your chicken from the butcher. This is a great dish when cooking for a large number of people as it looks after itself once it is in the oven.

SERVES 4

1 x 2k/4 ½ lb chicken, jointed
salt and black pepper
8 bay leaves
2 sprigs fresh rosemary
3 cloves garlic, 1 crushed, 2 sliced
½ bottle Chianti
1 to 2 tbsp flour
olive oil
6 anchovy fillets
2 tbsp olives, stoned
2 x 400g/14oz tins plum tomatoes

Preheat the oven to gas 4/180c.

Season the chicken pieces with salt and freshly ground black pepper. Put them in a bowl with the bay leaves, sprigs of rosemary, crushed clove of garlic and cover with the wine. Leave to marinate for at least an hour, but overnight if you have time, in the fridge.

Drain the chicken, reserving the marinade and pat dry with kitchen paper. Sprinkle the flour over the chicken. Heat a heavy pan and add the olive oil. Fry the chicken pieces until nicely brown in several batches and set aside. Using the same pan add the sliced garlic, fry for a few moments then add the anchovies, olives, tomatoes and finally put the chicken pieces back in too.

Pour in the marinade, bring to simmering point, cover and put into the oven for 1½ hours.

At the end of the cooking time, stir, taste and adjust the seasoning if required. Remove the bay leaves and rosemary and serve.

DINNER TUESDAY
anchored in
Loch Riddon.

prawn cocktail

salmon in Parmesan & parsley crust

Fresh fruit salad & Muscavado swirl

Baked Salmon with Parmesan and Parsley Crust

Fish must never be overcooked. It should always remain moist. This is a beautiful mixture of textures with the inner core of soft salmon, encrusted in a layer of crisp parmesan. Yet the cheese does not overpower the subtle flavour of the salmon.

SERVES 6

6 x 5oz/130g salmon fillets, skinned
salt and black pepper
butter if necessary
topping
1oz/25g fresh white breadcrumbs
1oz/25g Parmesan, coarsely grated
2 tbsp chopped fresh parsley
grated rind of ½ lemon
paprika
bunch fresh parsley, chopped

Preheat the oven to gas 7/220c.

Season both sides of the salmon fillets and place on baking parchment or arrange in a large buttered roasting tin.

In a bowl, mix the breadcrumbs, Parmesan, parsley and lemon rind for the topping and place this mixture on top of the salmon fillets, then sprinkle with a little paprika.

Bake for 10-15 minutes in the pre-heated oven.

When the salmon is done it will have changed from translucent to an opaque pink.

Sprinkle with more chopped parsley and serve immediately.

Fisherman's Pie

This recipe is a good excuse for eating anything that's been caught in the sea. So, don't be too precious about the exact ingredients. Be guided by what you've got. On the Puffer, contents have included langoustine, mussels and whatever the local fisherman has caught that day. However, having some smoked fish (preferably haddock, which is relatively firm) is important and turns the dish from just being 'fish pie' into something special.

SERVES 4

1½lbs/675g smoked and unsmoked fish
4oz/100g butter
1pt/600ml milk
2oz/50g plain flour
4oz/100g prawns, peeled
2 hardboiled eggs, roughly chopped
1 level tbsp capers
3 tbsp parsley, chopped
1 tbsp lemon juice
salt and pepper
For the topping
2lbs/900g freshly boiled potatoes
1oz/25g butter
¼pt/150ml natural yoghurt
a little freshly grated nutmeg

Preheat the oven to gas 6/200c.

Arrange the fish in a baking tin and season well with salt and pepper.

Pour on half of the milk, dot with a few flecks of butter and bake in the oven for 15 minutes.

Pour off and reserve the cooking liquid and flake the fish into bite-sized chunks (removing skin if necessary).

To make the white sauce: melt the rest of the butter, stir in the flour and cook for a few minutes. Slowly add the reserved milk, beating well to keep the sauce smooth. Then pour in the rest of the milk and season with salt and pepper.

Gently mix the fish into the sauce together with the prawns, hardboiled eggs, capers, parsley and lemon juice.

Mash the potatoes with the butter and yoghurt, add salt, pepper and a little nutmeg.

Spread the potato mixture over the fish, dot with the butter and bake for about half an hour until heated through and browned.

Tarte Tatin

This is the classic French dessert and equivalent to our apple pie. Where it differs is that the fruit is caramelised and the whole thing is upside down. It was invented in the 1890s by Stephanie Tatin at the hotel bearing her name. Interestingly, the Hotel Tatin is still going today. Tarte Tatin should be made with firm dessert apples. Cooking apples tend to mulch down into a purée.

SERVES 4–6

Pastry
4oz/100g plain flour
2oz/50g butter
a little cold water

Filling
4oz/100g soft dark brown sugar
1 tsp ground cinnamon
1lb/450g eating apples, peeled, cored and thinly sliced
1 tbsp butter for greasing the tin

Preheat the oven to gas 4/180c.

You will need an 8in/20cm sponge tin with straight sides, brushed with melted butter with the base covered with a piece of greaseproof paper which has been brushed with melted butter

First make the pastry by rubbing the butter into the flour until it looks like breadcrumbs. Now add a little water to bring the mixture together so leaving the sides of the mixing bowl clean. Roll this into a ball and put in a plastic bag in the fridge until needed.

Sprinkle the base of the tin with the sugar. Add the cinnamon and then arrange the apple slices neatly making sure everything is well pressed down.

Roll out the pastry to about ½ in/1cm thick and cut out a circle that will exactly fit the tin. Press the pastry gently down and place in the oven for about 40 minutes until the pastry is golden.

Take the tart out of the oven and set aside until it is completely cold. Now loosen the edges and carefully turn it upside down onto your serving plate.

Cranachan

It was Samuel Johnson, in his dictionary of 1755, who defined oats as "a grain, which in England is generally given to horses, but in Scotland supports the people". He had clearly never tried cranachan.

SERVES 4

3oz/75g medium oatmeal
7 tbsp whisky
3 tbsp honey
1pt/600ml double cream lightly whipped
    to the soft peak stage
1lb/450g raspberries

Toast the oatmeal in a frying pan being careful not to burn it. Set aside to cool.

Slowly and gently heat the honey and whisky together in a pan. Allow to cool.

Fold the whisky and honey mixture into the cream with the oatmeal and raspberries.

Serve in dessert glasses and garnish with a few raspberries.

Rhubarb and Ginger Crumble

This is the best of all crumbles. Rhubarb and ginger were made for each other and they taste perfect together in this dish. Rhubarb can be found almost anywhere, even on the west coast of Scotland.

SERVES 6

Filling
2lb/900g rhubarb
3oz/75g soft brown sugar
1 level tsp powdered ginger

Crumble
3oz/75g butter at room temperature
8oz/225g plain flour
5oz/130g soft brown sugar
1 level tsp baking powder

Preheat the oven to gas 4/180c.

Cut the rhubarb into chunks and place them in a saucepan together with the sugar and ginger. Cook over a gentle heat (covered) for about 15 minutes, stirring occasionally and to make sure the uncooked bits get down to the heat. Don't overcook. It should remain 'chunky'.

When cooked, drain off about half the juice and transfer the fruit to a pie-dish.

Make the crumble topping by rubbing the butter into the flour until it looks like fine breadcrumbs. Stir in the baking powder and sugar.

Sprinkle the rhubarb with crumble topping and bake for 30–40 minutes.

WHAT TO DO WITH THE RHUBARB LEAVES

Rhubarb leaves are poisonous but make a very effective natural pesticide for leaf eating insects. Simply put the leaves in a pan, cover with water and boil for about 20 minutes. When cool, add a teaspoonful of washing up liquid. When sprayed on roses it will kill greenfly.

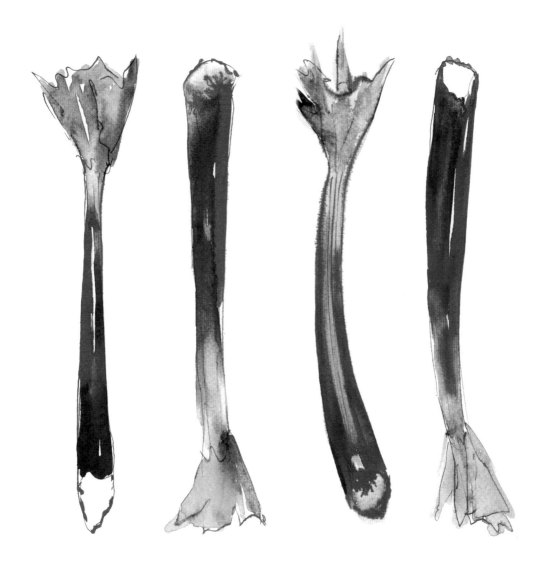

Plum Clafoutis

Very traditional, very French and very appropriate, given the close association between France and Scotland enshrined in 'the auld alliance'. The alliance dates from the treaty signed by John Balliol and Philip IV of France in 1295 against Edward I of England. The terms of which stipulated that if either country was attacked by England, the other country would invade English territory. It was the French too who helped Bonnie Prince Charlie escape from Skye and the clutches of the English by giving him safe passage on a French frigate.

SERVES 6

1lb/450g plums, halved and stones
    removed
2 large eggs
3oz/75g caster sugar
3 tbsp flour
¼ tsp salt (optional)
5fl oz/150ml double cream
½pt/300ml milk
3 tbsp kirsch or cognac

Preheat the oven to gas 5/190c.

Spread the plums over the base of a well buttered, shallow, ovenproof dish.

Put the eggs and sugar in a bowl and beat them thoroughly until thick and light. Add the flour then salt and beat until smooth. Gradually whisk in the cream, milk and kirsch to make a light batter.

Pour the batter over the plums and bake for 45 minutes or until set and brown on top.

Serve hot with cream or crème fraiche.

Chocolate Surprise Pudding

The 'surprise' in the pudding is that you make it with the sauce on the top and it ends up at the bottom when cooked. This high calorie pudding can be eaten relatively guilt-free if you exercise. On the Puffer, this is best done by stoking the boiler – two shovelfuls every five minutes will give six knots and a good appetite.

SERVES 4

Cake
3oz/75g self raising flour
2 level tsp cocoa powder
4oz/100g butter
4oz/100g caster sugar
2 eggs, beaten
½ tsp vanilla extract
1–2 tbsp milk

Sauce
4 oz/100g soft brown sugar
2 level tbsp cocoa powder
½pt/300ml hot water

Preheat the oven to gas 5/190c.

Sift the flour and the cocoa powder together and set aside.

Cream the butter and sugar until pale and light. Add the eggs and vanilla extract, little by little. Fold in the flour and cocoa. The mixture should be a soft consistency by now – if it is a little thick add some of the milk. Then spoon the mixture into a well-buttered 2½pt/1½l baking dish.

Now make the sauce. Put the soft brown sugar and cocoa powder into a mixing basin. Add the hot water and mix thoroughly. Pour over the top of the cake mixture and place in the preheated oven for 40 minutes.

Serve with cream or crème fraiche.

The most useful knot is the bowline. Learn to tie it with your eyes shut in case you need one in the dark.

NICK WALKER

Raising the anchor with the steam winch.

Key Lime Cheesecake

Two puddings – so easy to make.

SERVES 8-10

Base
3oz/75g butter
9oz/250g ginger biscuits, crushed

Filling
2 x 7oz/200g tubs full fat soft cheese
14oz/397g can Carnation Condensed Milk
4 limes, finely grated zest and juice

To finish
1 lime, thinly sliced

You will need a 9in/23cm spring-form cake tin.

Melt the butter and stir in the crushed biscuits. Press onto the base of the cake tin and chill for 10–15 minutes.

In a large bowl, whisk together the soft cheese, condensed milk, lime zest and juice until thick and glossy. Spoon this mixture over the biscuit base and chill for at least an hour but preferably overnight.

Just before serving, remove the cheesecake from the tin and place on a serving plate. Decorate with the lime slices and serve.

Tangy Lemon Pudding

SERVES 6

½pt/300ml double cream
2 tsp lemon zest
1oz/25g almonds, ground
3 tbsp lemon juice
2 oz/50g caster sugar
lemon zest for decoration

Put all the ingredients into a bowl and whisk until thick and light.

Spoon into individual glasses or ramekins, decorate with a little lemon zest and serve with vanilla biscuits (see page 122).

Fiddlers on board.

Vanilla Biscuits

MAKES ABOUT 20 BISCUITS.

4oz/125g butter, softened
2½oz/60g caster sugar
few drops vanilla extract
5oz/130g plain flour, sieved
caster sugar for sprinkling on the top

Preheat the oven to gas 4/180c.

Put the butter in a bowl and beat. Add the sugar and continue to beat until creamy. Now add the vanilla and the flour and stir them into the creamed mixture. Once you have thickish, well mixed dough, turn it onto a floured work surface and briefly knead.

Roll to about ¼in/6mm thick and using a 2in/5cm cutter cut out the biscuits. Put them onto a greased baking tray and cook for 10–12 minutes until they are pale golden and crisp.

Remove for the oven and sprinkle with the extra caster sugar before lifting them onto a wire rack to cool completely.

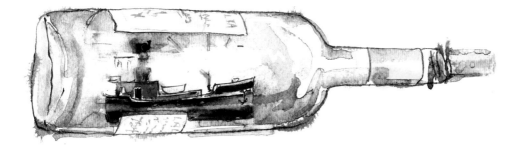

Bread and Butter Pudding

A classic pudding. Make it a bit more original though by using pannetone, brioche, hot cross buns or any other bread that takes your fancy.

SERVES 4–6

8 slices bread, buttered
2oz/50g currants
1 tbsp marmalade
½ pt/300ml milk
5fl oz/150ml double cream
grated rind of ½ lemon
2oz/50g caster sugar
3 eggs
Nutmeg, grated
butter for greasing

Preheat the oven to gas 4/180c.

You will need a 2pt/1l shallow baking dish.

Butter the baking dish. Cut each slice of buttered bread in half. Arrange 4 of these slices in one layer over the bottom of the dish – you may need to cut the bread a bit more to get a nice even covering. Sprinkle on half the currants and all the marmalade. Now cover with the rest of the bread and the remaining currants.

Put the milk and cream into a jug. Stir in the caster sugar and lemon peel.

Whisk the eggs in a separate bowl and then add them to the milk mixture. Pour this over the bread and sprinkle some grated nutmeg over the surface. Push the bread under the surface adding a little more milk and cream if necessary.

Bake in the oven for 30–40 minutes.

A five minute job is one that you assume will take five minutes. Usually it takes days.

NICK WALKER

Opposite: Moored at Tarbert.

Summer Pudding

Soft fruit grows very well, all over Scotland. This pudding is best made with various combinations of raspberries, strawberries, redcurrants and blackcurrants. However, be careful not to use too many blackcurrants as they tend to dominate the flavour.

SERVES 6

1lb/450g raspberries
8oz/225g redcurrants
4oz/100g blackcurrants
5oz/130g caster sugar
7–8 slices white bread

You will need a 1½pt/850ml pudding basin, buttered.

Put the fruits and sugar into a pan and cook them slowly for a few minutes until the sugar has melted and juice starts to flow. Remove from the heat and set aside.

Now carefully line the pudding basin with the bread overlapping each piece slightly to make sure there are no gaps. As you come to the top let pieces of the bread hang over the rim – they will be used later to fold over the top of the pudding.

Pour the fruit into the bread lined basin. It should be almost up to the top by now. Keep some of the juice back – this will be added just before serving. Fold over the pieces of bread and top with a final slice of bread to ensure the whole pudding is totally enclosed with bread. Fit a saucer or plate on top of the pudding so that it rests on the pudding rather than the rim. Place some weights (tinned tomatoes are perfect) on the plate and put in the fridge overnight.

Just before serving turn the pudding onto a serving dish and pour over the reserved juice to cover any patches of bread which are still white.

Serve with cream or ice cream.

Harbour light at Crinan.

Jura Blackcurrant Mousse

This recipe is made on Jura in August with blackcurrants from Neil's croft. Neil is the piper who, with friends, entertains Puffer passengers with musical evenings when the VIC 32 is tied up at Craighouse. The mousse can, of course, be made anywhere, but the blackcurrants, like the midges, are larger on Jura.

SERVES 6

1lb/450g blackcurrants
4oz/100g caster sugar
15fl oz/450ml double cream*
1 sachet vegetarian gelatine

*A low-fat alternative for this recipe is to substitute Greek yoghurt in place of the double cream.

De-stalk and wash the fruit before placing in a pan with the sugar and heat gently until soft and the sugar is dissolved. Then sieve the resulting fruit pulp to remove the seeds and skins. Cool for 15 minutes.

Dissolve the gelatine in a small amount of blackcurrant puree and when cool add the rest of the puree. Whip the cream into snowy peaks and then fold in to the blackcurrant puree. Transfer the mixture into six dessert dishes and place in the fridge.

Garnish with small piece of fresh mint. Serve chilled.

Opposite: Clouds and smoke off Largs.

Caramel Ice Cream

If you've never had this ice cream, it might sound rather bizarre. Caramelised breadcrumbs add a delicious nuttiness. In fact, it encapsulates everything that's good about brown bread and cream. Flecked with crunchy sweet nuggets, it's a party in your mouth and all your taste buds are invited.

SERVES 6–8

3oz/75g fresh brown breadcrumbs
2oz/50g Demerara sugar
4 eggs, separated
4oz/100g caster sugar
½pt/300ml double cream

Put the breadcrumbs and Demerara sugar on an enamel or foil plate and toast under a hot grill until golden brown and caramelised, stirring occasionally. This will take 5–8 minutes. Leave to become quite cold.

Whisk the egg yolks in a small bowl until well blended.

In another, larger bowl whisk the egg whites until stiff and then whisk in the caster sugar a teaspoon at a time.

Whisk the cream until it forms soft peaks and then fold into the meringue mixture with the egg yolks and caramelised breadcrumbs. Pour into a 2½pt/1½l rigid container. Cover and freeze.

Before serving bring to room temperature for 5 minutes. Serve with biscuits.

Superb Carrot Cake

It's surprising to find something that calls itself a cake which contains more fruit and vegetables than the average greengrocer. However, it works. And the carrot and banana give it a beautifully succulent, moist texture.

8oz/225g self raising flour
2 level tsp baking powder
5oz/150g light muscovado sugar
4oz/100g carrots, coarsely grated
2 ripe bananas, mashed
2 eggs
5fl oz/150ml sunflower oil
2oz/50g walnuts, shelled and chopped
Topping
8oz/225g cream cheese (Philadelphia)
3oz/75g butter, softened
6oz/175g icing sugar, sifted
a little vanilla extract

Preheat the oven to gas 4/180c.

Line a small roasting tin (6½in x 10½in/17cm x 28cm) with foil and grease it well.

Measure all the cake ingredients except the walnuts into a bowl. Beat well until smooth and then stir in the nuts. Pour into the prepared tin.

Bake in the oven for 45–50 minutes until the cake is well risen, golden-brown and firm to the touch.

Take out of the oven, cool and then turn out onto a tray or board and remove the foil.

Put all the topping ingredients into a bowl and beat until smooth. Spread this over the cake.

You must, as a Captain, encourage initiative; because if you think you are going to be able to make all the decisions and do everything yourself, you become exhausted very quickly, incapable soon after and a wreck shortly after that.

NICK WALKER

Sticky Gingerbread with Lemon Icing

The design on the tin of Lyle's treacle, unchanged since 1885, is possibly the oldest in Britain. Along with most Puffers, Abram Lyle was born on the Clyde (at Greenock) where he started a shipping fleet, transporting sugar. He was a deeply religious man, hence the biblical quotation, which you can still see on the tin today. It comes from the story of Samson who, on a journey through the land of the Philistines, killed a lion. Later, returning past the same spot, and seeing there was honey and a swarm of bees in the carcass, he said: "Out of the eater came forth meat and out of the strong came forth sweetness".

8oz/225g plain flour
3oz/75g soft brown sugar
1 tsp bicarbonate of soda
2 tsp ground ginger
2 tsp cinnamon
2 tsp mixed spice
pinch of salt
2½oz/60g margarine
4fl oz/110ml milk
1 tbsp golden syrup
3 tbsp treacle
Icing
4oz/100g icing sugar
lemon juice

Preheat the oven to gas 4/180c.

You will need a 9in x 5in/23cm x 13cm loaf tin, buttered, lined with baking paper and buttered again.

Put all the dry ingredients into a bowl and give them a stir.

Warm the milk together with the margarine, syrup and treacle, stirring thoroughly, then add to dry ingredients and mix well.

Pour everything into the well-greased loaf tin and bake for about 40 minutes. The gingerbread will be well risen when it comes out of the oven before it sinks like mad but that's fine because it turns out nice and squidgy.

Once the gingerbread is cool, mix the icing sugar with a little lemon juice until it is runny. Now spread the icing over the gingerbread, wait a few minutes before removing from the tin and peeling the greaseproof paper off.

Slice and serve.

Coaling at Tarbert.

One-way Flapjacks

The name 'one-way' refers to this recipe's remarkable ability to stay down even in the roughest sea conditions.

MAKES 24 SQUARES

2oz/50g demerara sugar
2oz/50g soft brown sugar
3oz/75g butter
2oz/50g golden syrup
7oz/200g rolled oats

Preheat the oven to gas 3/170c.

Heat all the ingredients except the oats in a large saucepan until the sugar has melted. Take saucepan off the heat and stir in the oats.

Press the mixture into a baking tray with a palette knife or the back of a spoon.

Bake for 15-20 minutes, remove from oven and leave to cool for 10 minutes.

Mark into 24 squares and leave to finish cooling in the tin.

Looking across Loch Linnhe from Appin.

Scones

There are two things that the Puffer engineer cooks better than anyone else: bacon and eggs, fried on a shovel in the boiler fire and . . . scones. As not many homes have the wherewithal to do the former, we thought that his recipe for scones would be more appropriate.

MAKES ABOUT 12

8oz/225g plain flour
3 tsp baking powder
pinch of salt
1½ oz/40g butter
5fl oz/150ml milk

Mix the salt and baking powder into the flour. Rub the butter into the flour until it's like fine breadcrumbs. Make a well in the flour and pour in the milk. Mix into soft dough using a cold knife. Turn out onto floured board and knead for five minutes and then pat into an oval shape approximately 1 inch thick. Cut into squares or portions depending on how greedy you are! Brush top of scones with a little milk and place on tray and bake at 200c for 12–15 minutes until straw-coloured on top. Allow to cool on a wire rack and serve with Cornish clotted cream and your finest homemade jam.

Coffee and Walnut Traybake

MAKES ABOUT 21 PIECES

8oz/225g softened butter
8oz/225g light muscovado sugar
10oz/275g self-raising flour
2 level tsp baking powder
4 large eggs
2 tbsp coffee essence (Camp Coffee)
3oz/75g chopped walnuts

For the icing
3oz/75g softened butter
8oz/225g sifted icing sugar
2 tsp milk
2 tsp coffee essence
Walnut halves

Preheat the oven to gas 4/180c.

Grease a 12 x 9in/30 x 23cm traybake or roasting tin, line base with baking parchment.

Measure all cake ingredients into large bowl and beat until well blended. Turn mixture into prepared tin and level the top.

Bake in preheated oven for about 35-40 minutes or until the cake has shrunk from sides of tin and springs back when pressed in the centre with your fingertips. Leave to cool in tin.

To make the icing

Beat together the butter, icing sugar, milk and coffee essence. Spread evenly over the cold cake using a palette knife, then decorate with walnut halves and cut into 21 pieces.

Opposite: Ben More.

Crinan Fruit Cake with Ginger

Makes as many pieces as there are people for tea.

1 lb/450g mixed fruit and nuts, such as
  apricots, cherries, raisins, sultanas and
  nuts, roughly chopped
4oz/100g butter
1 tsp bicarbonate of soda
6oz/175g light muscovado sugar
8fl oz/250ml water
2 eggs, beaten
10oz/275g self-raising flour
2 tsp ground ginger
4-6 oz/100–175g stem ginger, drained
  and roughly chopped

Preheat the oven to gas 3/170c.

Grease and line a 8in/20cm deep round
cake tin.

Put the prepared fruits and nuts, butter,
bicarbonate of soda, sugar and water into
a large pan. Bring to the boil, stirring
constantly and boil for three minutes. Allow
to cool.

Now add the eggs, flour, ground ginger and
stem ginger. Mix thoroughly and turn into
the prepared cake tin and smooth the top.

Bake for about 1¼–1½ hours or until a
skewer inserted into the centre comes out
clean and the cake is firm to the touch.

Cool before turning the cake out onto a
wire rack.

Chocolate Beer Cake

Unlikely but delicious. Surprise yourself and your crew by baking this for afternoon tea. Then sit back and listen to the sighs of satisfaction before they all fall asleep.

4oz/100g butter or margarine
10oz/275g dark soft brown sugar
2 eggs, beaten
6oz/175g plain flour
¼ tsp baking powder
1 tsp bicarbonate of soda
7fl oz/200ml sweet stout
2oz/50g cocoa

Icing
4oz/100g plain chocolate
2 tbsp sweet stout
2oz/50g butter
4oz/100g icing sugar, sifted

To decorate
grated chocolate

Preheat the oven to gas 4/180c.

You will need 2 x 8in/20cm sandwich tins, greased and bases lined with baking parchment.

Cream together the butter and sugar until they become pale and fluffy. Now gradually beat in the eggs, stirring well between each addition.

In a separate bowl, mix the flour, baking powder and bicarbonate of soda.

In another bowl (or jug) mix the cocoa with the sweet stout.

Now, fold a little of the flour mixture into the creamed butter and sugar, then add a little of the cocoa mixture. Continue adding and folding until everything has been incorporated.

Divide the mixture between the 2 sandwich tins and bake for 30–35 minutes. Leave the cakes to cool in the tin for a few minutes before turning onto a wire rack.

When the cakes are cool you can make the icing by placing the chocolate and the stout in a bowl and setting it over a pan of barely simmering water. Once the chocolate has melted, stir in the butter. Leave the mixture to cool for a moment before adding the sugar and beat this in too.

Use half the icing to sandwich the cake together and the rest to cover the top and sides. Finally grate some flakes of chocolate over the top.

Lemon Drizzle Cake

Puffer cooks need only bring the lemons, in the knowledge that the West Coast will provide the drizzle.

SERVES ... QUITE A FEW AND EVEN MORE WHEN IT'S DRIZZLING.

12oz/350g butter
12oz/350g soft brown sugar
12oz/350g self-raising flour
4 eggs–beaten
grated rind of 2 lemons
Icing
8oz/225g icing sugar
juice of 2 lemons

Preheat the oven to gas 4/180c.

You will need 2 loaf tins, lined and buttered.

Melt the butter and sugar gently over a low heat. Take the pan off the heat and stir in the flour, eggs and lemon rind.

Divide this mixture between the 2 loaf tins. Bake for 25-30 minutes or until a skewer comes out clean.

Leave the cakes to cool in the tins for a few minutes and make the icing.

Sieve the icing sugar into a bowl and add just enough lemon juice to allow the mixture to become spreadable. Now divide the icing between the 2 cakes. Cover them and then wait for the cake to cool completely before cutting into slices.

If you don't like the weather on the west coast, just wait half an hour.

Loch Oich.

Everyday Granary Bread

Each morning on the Puffer the cook makes the bread for the day for passengers and crew. It's not difficult to make bread but it is critical to get the rising right. To test the dough, depress two fingers into the centre and if the dent stays, it has risen sufficiently. Letting the dough rise a second time before shaping will give a finer textured loaf.

Makes 1 large or 2 smaller loaves

1lb 2oz/500g granary flour
One sachet of instant yeast
1 tsp of sugar
1 tsp salt
3–4 tbsp olive oil
10fl oz/300ml warm water
a little extra oil for greasing the baking
    sheet or loaf tin

Optional:
handful of oatmeal
handful of sunflower seeds
handful of pine nuts

Preheat the oven to gas 8/230c.

Mix all the dry ingredients together and stir. Now rub in the olive oil. Add the warm water and the seeds and nuts if using them. Mix into a soft dough and knead for 10 minutes on a floured surface then put the ball of dough into a bowl and cover with a damp tea towel or piece of cling film. Leave in a warm place for up to one hour to allow it to rise to about twice its volume.

Tip the dough out. Give it a gentle knead and then form into the required shape or put it into 2 well greased loaf tins. Cover with the damp tea towel again and leave to rise for a second time for about 45 minutes or until it's about twice the size.

Put the bread into the oven for 30–35 minutes. Take the bread out of the oven and remove from the tray/loaf tin. Now turn it upside down and tap it; it should sound hollow if cooked.

Place on a wire rack to cool.

*Look out of the window at all times. Don't get bogged
down in petty details in chart work or satellite navigators
or the newspaper or any other thing that might distract
your attention from this vital task that you are paid to do.
Look out of the window.*

NICK WALKER

We saw a Minke whale off Eilean Mhor in the Sound of Jura. Somebody had noticed a lot of seabirds wheeling about and screaming over what looked like a rock. The rock moved and became the gaping jaws of a hungry whale, a rather untidy eater as he gulped vast quantities of fish, the seagulls fighting over his leftovers.

NICK WALKER

Seaweed Bread

Nearly all types of seaweed are edible, even bladder wrack; and the uses of kelp are protean, ranging from giving ice cream and toothpaste a smooth texture to giving a good 'head' to beer. Sea lettuce is one of the commoner varieties of seaweed. It can be eaten raw in salads, cooked in soups or used in bread, as in this recipe.

Makes 1 large loaf

1lb 2oz/500g strong white bread flour
1 sachet dried yeast
¼ tsp salt
4oz/100g seaweed lettuce/*ulva lactuca*, thoroughly rinsed and roughly chopped
4 tbsp olive oil
a little warm water to mix to a soft dough
a little extra oil for greasing the baking sheet/loaf tin

Preheat the oven to gas 8/230c.

First mix the dry ingredients together and then add the seaweed.

Mix in the olive oil and warm water to make a soft, pliable dough. Now knead for 10 minutes or so.

Put back into the bowl and cover with either a damp tea towel or a sheet of cling film. Leave in a warm place to double in size for about an hour.

Tip the dough out gently and briefly knead again. Now place on a greased baking sheet or put into a greased 1lb loaf tin. Leave to rise for a further 40 minutes.

Bake for 30–35 minutes or until the loaf sounds hollow when it is tapped on the bottom.

Olive Bread

As a vehicle for other foods, bread is possibly the most versatile. In this form, the addition of olive oil and mint transports you to somewhere about 5 miles offshore from Nice or Cannes. Despite the weather, this gives passengers aboard the Puffer the illusion that they are cruising towards Cap Antibes rather than Rothesay or Arran.

MAKES 1 LARGE LOAF

1lb/450g strong white flour

1 packet dried yeast

3 tbsp olive oil

1 medium onion, finely chopped and
    softened in olive oil

1 tbsp fresh mint, chopped

a little warm water

salt and pepper

4oz/100g pitted olives, finely chopped

Preheat the oven to gas 8/230c.

Mix the flour with the yeast. Stir in first the olive oil and then add the water so that the dough comes together. Add the cooked onion, salt and mint.

Knead for about 10 minutes until soft and elastic and then add olives. Put into a bowl and cover with a damp tea towel or clingfilm and leave to double in size.

Tip the dough out and knead again gently. Form a domed shape with the dough and put onto a baking tray or divide between 2 loaf tins. Cover.

Allow to rise again for 20-30 minutes before cooking for about 30 minutes.

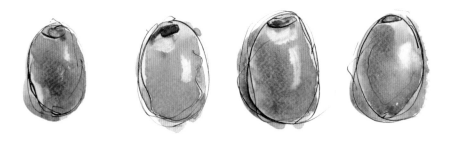

Opposite: Evening in Loch Melfort.

Index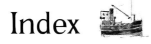